STUNNING

BY

CATHERINE RYMSHA

Stunning
© 2021 Catherine M. Rymsha. All rights reserved.

This book is designed to provide information and inspiration to readers. It is sold with the understanding that the publisher and author are not engaged to render any type of psychological, legal, or any other kind of professional or career advice. The content is the sole expression and opinion of the author. No warranties or guarantees are expressed or implied by the publisher's choice to include any of the content in this volume. Neither the publisher nor the author shall be liable for any physical, psychological, emotional, financial, or commercial damages, including, but not limited to, special, incidental, consequential, or other damages. The names of participants in the story have been masked to preserve privacy.

ISBN: 978-1-7357313-3-9 (paperback)
ISBN: 978-1-7357313-4-6 (ebook)

Cover and interior design by MiblArt.
Editorial services by Susan McGrath

Published by The Leadership Decision
www.TheLeadershipDecision.com

BIO

Catherine Rymsha is the author of *The Leadership Decision*, which builds on her TEDx Talk. She is a leadership development expert, both in her professional and academic backgrounds. She currently teaches at the University of Massachusetts, Lowell. Her second book, *Stunning*, stems from her fascination with murder mystery documentaries and crimes stories.

Catherine is from West Newbury, Massachusetts. She received an Master of Science and Doctor of Education in leadership from Northeastern University and a Bachelor of Arts in English and communications from the Massachusetts College of Liberal Arts in North Adams. She enjoys spending time with her dog, Mia, vacationing in Nantucket, and running.

CHAPTER 1

NEWBURYPORT, MASSACHUSETTS

Saturday, May 8, at 3:43 p.m.

There wasn't anything special about Caroline and Greg's life together. A word she used with friends to sum it up was "ordinary." But one day, it changed. And not in the way that some people's lives change with a new job or by having a baby. It changed in the way that it could never, and would never, go back to normal.

It started by Caroline simply taking the dog for a walk. Specifically, she took her dog, Rose, to the river across the street from her home in Newburyport, Massachusetts, to let the dog swim.

Caroline brought Rose's ball and threw it in the water countless times. Between tosses, she noticed the current was flowing upriver and the wind was strong, whipping her short blond hair around her face. She watched the buoys get knocked over then swoop back up violently against the surf. For a moment, she wondered if the current was too strong. But after each throw, she watched Rose's head bob in the water, marked by a neon-green flash of her collar, as she fought her way back to shore.

Their outing must have lasted no more than fifteen minutes. Or so her memory, which has been tested more than a hundred times, reminds her.

Caroline had glanced at her watch before leaving. It had been 3:43 p.m. as they stepped into the gray May afternoon, leaving Greg and her best friend, Noel, behind in the house. Noel was sitting in the screened, three-season room that abutted the kitchen. She was wrapped in an old blanket that Caroline had had since college in Amherst. It was pea-green, fuzzy, and silly, but warm.

A half hour earlier, Greg had hovered between the kitchen and the sliding glass door.

"Do you both want wine?" he asked.

"Man, of course we do!" yelled Noel, slapping her thigh.

He walked back to the kitchen for a few moments and then came back empty-handed.

"Greg, where's the wine?" Caroline asked.

"Oh, I forgot all about it," he said and rubbed his face. He was still handsome like he had been in college.

His green eyes darted from Caroline to Noel and then back to Caroline.

"He's so distracted these days, especially today," Caroline had said, turning to Noel. "I can't understand why."

When Caroline got back, she glanced at her watch again. It was now 3:56 p.m. Greg and Noel were not where she had left them, and the sliding glass door was open. This was surprising since it was usually stuck shut, especially in the early spring nights in New England with the moisture in the air. As she came closer to the door, she noticed a scratch next to the wooden frame as if a knife had grazed the white paint ever so slightly, leaving a slight orange tinge behind.

Caroline called out to her husband. No answer. She called out to her friend. No answer.

Suddenly, the house felt heavy like the current. Gray. She felt a tingle begin in the small of her back and move like lightning throughout her body. She knew something was wrong. She called for her husband again and surprised herself with the fear she heard in her voice. She put her hand on the table to steady herself, but her feet felt as if they were glued to the ground.

Caroline yelled for both. Still no answer. She called his name again. "Greg?" She said it again. And then again. She said it slowly, feeling the *g*, the *r*, the *e*, and the last *g* fall from her tongue.

Her tone was almost that of an animal suffering. Shrill. Rose's ears perked as she sensed something was wrong. Caroline slid carefully around the counter into the kitchen and throughout the first floor of the house, peering around each corner like something was going to grab her.

The next nonsensical thing she remembered saying, and not so much saying as shrieking in a tone she had never heard or thought she would make, was, "Noel!"

CHAPTER 2

CAROLINE AND GREG

How it began

Caroline met Greg in their senior year of college after her breakup with Matt. To this day when Caroline heard the name Matt, she would look around optimistically thinking that maybe *her* Matt would be standing there. He was the one she had hoped for all along.

She thought that over time she would feel for Greg the way she felt for Matt, but it never happened. She loved him, but it was never the love she hoped it would be.

When Greg got down on one knee, she said yes. She still didn't even know why. No one ever prepares you for that moment. She wasn't pregnant, and there was no one dying in the family who wanted to see her wed, but she still said yes. Her head told her he would be a good partner. He didn't really drink, didn't use drugs, and she had never suspected him of cheating. Caroline rationalized it and thought, "Okay, so this is it. This will be the rest of my life."

She was walked down the aisle by both her mother and father. She looked at Greg as she made her way down the aisle and saw his shoulders widen as he breathed in. She tried to take a mental picture of him in that moment. That was decades ago. Through the years, the two had aged well. Greg looked the same with his brown hair and green eyes.

He had a charm about him. He did. And he was kind. He played lacrosse in college and kept his athletic build throughout the years. He majored in political science and minored in biology. And now, years later, he had established himself as vice president of sales for a medical device company. Caroline, who majored in journalism and started her career in freelancing and publishing, was now working part-time writing for a local paper.

On their third date, Greg picked her up in his Jeep and took them to play miniature golf. He fumbled with the stick shift, making the car stall in the middle of the street. She laughed nervously and waved for cars to pass. Caroline tried not to be embarrassed but she was. She thought about Matt and how he shifted his Jeep seamlessly.

When Matt took her out for the first time, Caroline hopped into his Jeep, which was the only similarity between Greg and Matt, he put his arm around her, pulled her in tight, and kissed her. It was electric. One weekend, for their third date, they drove hours to Cape Cod just to get oysters and cold beers.

But before she knew it, Caroline was getting married to Greg and wondering if she was making the right decision. She couldn't go back, or so she thought.

Things moved quickly after that. Scarily so. Her time with Matt felt like a dream. She and Greg inherited their house in Newburyport from his aunt. Grad school came and went. Full-time jobs were started, children arrived, and life settled down just fine.

CHAPTER 3

UNIVERSITY OF MASSACHUSETTS, AMHERST, MASSACHUSETTS

Caroline, Greg, and Noel, thirty-two years ago

Noel was the one who made Greg seem special at first. They had been friends all throughout college. Nothing had ever happened between them, Greg told Caroline after a few dates. Except for one time, over a bottle of cheap wine, they shared a kiss.

"I always want to be honest with you," he told her, his strong hands gripping hers.

"I'm glad," she replied. She already knew, though. Noel had told her. Yet, it was still nice to hear from Greg to help build their trust. Knowing that information did make her uneasy, but she told herself to suck it up, to be an adult and get over it. Yet she still asked them both about it separately here and there over the years. The story was always the same.

A part of Caroline cared, mostly because of her relationship with Noel, but a larger part of her didn't. Who cared if they had kissed decades earlier? He married Caroline, not Noel, so why should it even matter?

The kiss came after Greg had achieved something with lacrosse—Caroline couldn't even remember what exactly. Some sort of championship or something. Noel had a bottle of wine left over from a sorority party. They sat in Noel's college apartment talking about his "big win," Noel listening patiently and waiting to share her story about her new and first girlfriend.

Their kiss happened for only a few seconds. That was it. So ordinary, too. Not even ordinary. It was bland, as Noel had described it. Caroline thought it sounded like Greg through and through and completely unlike what she would expect from wild and passionate Noel.

Caroline brought up the kiss in fits of rage and frustration when she felt Greg wasn't being aggressive enough at work or strict enough with their children, but she never *really* cared. It was something to pick at when she wanted to start a fight.

"Do you love Noel?" Caroline had screamed at him once when he was late coming home from work.

"No, I do not," he said calmly. "I love you. I always have."

This was his typical response whenever she brought up Noel and the kiss. Yet Caroline always cared deeply about Noel. Noel had a fire in her next to which Caroline smoldered. She knew it, Noel knew it, everyone knew it. Noel was average height. She fit directly under Caroline's chin. Even with heels on at college parties, she could never meet Caroline eye to eye. The only time they were head to head was when they were lying in bed watching TV.

Noel had curves and fiery red hair with curls that hit at the cusp of her shoulders. Sometimes, Noel would lay her hair next to Caroline's when they were lounging in bed and talk about how funny Caroline would look with Noel's curly red hair framing her face.

The first night Caroline met Greg, he was standing next to Noel at a bar. Noel was taking whiskey shots while he nervously scanned the room and sipped a beer.

"Hey, girl," Noel said when Caroline came up behind her. "How are you? How's life? This is Greg."

Greg had smiled and nodded, but before Caroline could respond, Noel grabbed her hand and dragged her to the dance floor. Dancing like this was not normal for Caroline. Her ballet body tried to sway and groove in line with Noel's curves.

Noel made fun of Caroline the entire time and, for the first time in Caroline's life, she tried to laugh at herself and be okay with it even though she wanted to crumple to the floor because of embarrassment and the lingering sadness from a fallout with Matt hours prior.

Noel and Caroline stayed friends through the years. Caroline didn't know if it was only because of Greg, since those two continued on with their own friendship, too. But Caroline bonded more with Noel than she had ever bonded with anyone else, despite never openly admitting it. That would make her look too vulnerable.

Noel was the first visitor to her and Greg's first post-college apartment in Boston, and she stood like a soldier next to Caroline when she said her vows. When Caroline and Greg moved into their Newburyport house, Noel was again the first visitor. When she arrived, she and Caroline walked across the street to look at the river.

"Let's jump in," Noel said.

"No, it's so dirty," Caroline squealed.

"Fuck it," Noel replied and, with a running start, jumped in clothing and all.

Caroline had no choice but to follow Noel. She took her shoes off, put a toe in, and then pulled it out. She waded in cautiously up to her waist. Greg came over a few minutes later. He shook his head then sat down on the grassy spot next to the boat ramp with a beer in hand and watched the two women.

As soon as he sat, Noel ran out of the water, jumped squarely on him, and straddled his chest, soaking his shirt and making Caroline question that kiss from so many years ago. Caroline forced a laugh to cover her uneasiness in the moment. This was just Noel. Greg pushed Noel off to establish a boundary in front of his wife and in the looming eyes of their new home. Noel ran back to Caroline in the water.

The next day Noel left for Paris for three months to spend time with her mother and sister. Caroline settled in to married life and brushed off the idea of anything more than this ordinary existence that the average American dreams of having.

CHAPTER 4

NEWBURYPORT, MASSACHUSETTS

Saturday, May 8, at 4:21 p.m.

Rose and Caroline slowly worked their way down the hall trying to figure out if this was some weird joke or not. Caroline took a step. Then another.

"Noel, is this a joke?" she asked. No answer.

"Greg, where are you?" she then asked, assuming Noel talked him into hiding like children.

Sliding her phone out of her back pocket, her fingers frantically darted around the screen, first pushing on Greg's number. The phone rang, but no answer—just voicemail after a few rings. She hung up and her finger navigated to Noel's number. She pushed on it, and it went right to voicemail.

With no answer from either and still convinced this could possibly be a joke, she continued creeping through the house. No one in the living room or the office. Nor in the downstairs bathroom or guest room where Noel's stuff was scattered around the room. Traveling up the stairs, she called their names again. No answer. She checked her and Greg's bedroom. No one.

She checked the bathrooms and behind shower curtains and then the three other bedrooms on the second floor. Faces of family, friends, and pets from over the years smiled down on her from the walls as she moved from room to room. On the third floor, she navigated around the family room to the window that overlooked the river. The current was still strong. The river still looked gray.

She wondered why she was feeling so scared when she had no real reason to be afraid yet. But she was. She was more afraid than at any other time in her life. The anguish was like nothing she had ever felt before. She walked down the stairs to the hallway on the second floor and lay down on the floor.

As she stared up at the ceiling, Rose hovered over her, licking her face. She'd never lay on the floor before, especially in the hallway, surprising both herself and the dog. Rose didn't know what was wrong but her rough tongue licked Caroline's face in comfort. Caroline used the cuff on her sleeve to wipe where Rose had licked.

Caroline shut her eyes and decided that maybe Greg and Noel went for a walk. She nestled on the floor and tried to force her mind into that space between sleep and awake. Moments later, her mind sharpened to reality and for a moment she assumed they were now home and her moment of panic had been just a misunderstanding.

Getting up from the floor, she called their names again. Nothing. She walked downstairs and called their names again. Nothing. She moved through the sliding door frame and by the scratch, calling their names as she went. Nothing.

Stepping into the backyard, she called again. Still nothing. Then she heard someone call her name. It was familiar and a voice she knew, but not one she was calling for.

"Caroline, is everything okay?" a voice inquired.

Caroline turned to see who was speaking. Molly and her husband, Frank, her neighbors, were standing by the fence that separated their yards. In the late afternoon hours, they looked younger than sixty but concerned.

"Caroline, did you hear me?" Molly yelled again.

"Yes, I'm sorry. I just woke up from a nap," Caroline told the couple. "Have you seen Greg and my friend, Noel?"

"I think I saw them out here earlier. Yes, a few hours ago," Frank said as he reached for the fence post for support.

"They were out here for a moment, I think," he told her and then paused. "I think I saw them again maybe like an hour or so ago."

He was never the best communicator. Caroline learned that years ago when they were trying to put up the fence and he wouldn't answer direct questions like, "Will you help pay for this?" or "When can you get me the check that you promised?"

The couple had money and family who visited often from Boston. Yet, the family members who came from the city on holidays weren't upstanding like Frank and Molly. She knew this from overhearing family fights.

Frank's responses were always gray, unhelpful. Caroline learned, though, from the fence experience, to find ways to be more direct with him. She triggered her questions like a gun aiming for a target. "You're sure you saw them today?" followed by, "And you saw them both?" and lastly, "Around what time specifically? An hour ago, you said?"

"Yes, I'm sure it was today. Right, Molly? You saw them, too," he said. Molly nodded, her red curls bobbing up and down.

"Yup, it was both of them. They waved, and I always remember that Noel. She's quite the firecracker. She kind of looks like you," Frank said as he looked at his wife. Both of them chuckled.

"I always thought that Greg looks like you. And obviously when you were much younger, more handsome and taller," Molly jabbed back. The two chuckled again.

"Wait, what time is it now?" asked Caroline, getting impatient.

Molly glanced at her watch. "4:51."

Frank looked beyond Caroline at the house behind her.

"Well, one of the grandkids called me around the time I saw them," he said. "Damn kids looking for money again. Let me get the phone. These stupid things nowadays..."

Frank reached toward his pocket, his shaky hands trying to pull the phone out. Molly reached down to help her husband.

"Watch those hands," he said, trying to flirt and winking at Caroline. He looked at the phone and Molly pointed at it.

"3:45 p.m.," he said. "That's when I saw them outside here in the backyard, I think. But we've been in and out. But, Caroline, what's that over there?"

Caroline looked in the direction that Frank was pointing. There, in the yard, was Noel's white cellphone.

CHAPTER 5

MOUNT KATAHDIN, MAINE

Saturday, May 8, at 4:02 p.m.

Marigold did not live a life that anyone would envy. She was the last of five children and grew up in a mobile home in rural Maine near Big Moose Lake. Her father was a drunk, and her mother tried to provide the best life for the children that she could. None of them ventured far or outside of Maine. They all married young and had their own children near the shores of the lake, but Marigold decided to move closer to Mount Katahdin.

Marigold was short, under five feet tall, and thin. She had dark brown eyes that looked almost black and sharp features. Her looks, like her attitude, made people notice her yet fear her, too.

Marigold's daughter, Iris, arrived when Marigold was twenty-two. She had just started working at a local inn cleaning rooms. During her pregnancy, she would take her lunch break across the street from the inn, sitting by the dam and watching the water in the pond flow over its side. Behind her, two roads split, both leading to the mountain, one paved and one dirt.

Iris looked nothing like her mother. People often doubted that the two were even related. Iris was blond with blue eyes like her father. She was tall and heavyset. People didn't notice her the way they did her mother, but she was pretty with a full and kind face.

When Iris turned sixteen, she left town. Marigold knew she went out toward Boston to live and heard from her every few months. At twenty-two, Iris came back and cleaned rooms alongside her mother. They ate together by the dam at lunch.

Marigold told people that Iris always had the itch to leave. Iris always kicked in the womb and that's how Marigold knew that she wanted out. On the last day of August, six months after she'd arrived, Iris told her mother she was going back to Boston to be with her ex-boyfriend, Sammy.

Marigold met Sammy once. His frame was small and he was short, but his tattooed muscles were large from years of construction and heavy lifting. He had the face of a little boy with piercing green eyes that sometimes tinted yellow.

Iris welcomed twins almost a year later. Marigold and her friend drove all the way to Boston to see them. A boy, Harold, and a girl, Amelia. The twins looked like their mother with wide faces, blond hair, and blue eyes. They, too, were heavyset and challenged Marigold with carrying both at the same time. Two years later, the twins would be living with her in Maine while Iris stayed in the city with Sammy.

Marigold brought the children to school and tried to do more with them than she had done with her own child. The money that Iris sent monthly helped. After school each day, they'd go to the dam. The children would run around catching frogs and throwing sticks. It tuckered them out before heading home for homework and dinner. It was her favorite part of the day.

Marigold would take a drag from her flask and pray that the children would have better lives than she had and go to college and get good jobs and start families of their own who would be better off than them.

CHAPTER 6

NEWBURYPORT, MASSACHUSETTS

Saturday, May 8, at 6:43 p.m.

Caroline's hands shook as she picked up the telephone and dialed the number to the police station. She had called both Greg and Noel countless times at this point with no answer. Calling the police was now the only thing she could think to do. When the operator answered, she stayed on the line silent, not knowing what to say.

"Hello?" repeated the woman on the other end.

"Uh, yes. Hello. I think I'm calling to report a missing person. Or, persons, I mean." She paused and bit her thin bottom lip.

"Have they been gone more than twenty-four hours?" the woman asked.

"No, only a few hours. But I think something's wrong," Caroline replied.

"Ma'am, are they under the age of eighteen?" inquired the operator.

"No," Caroline answered.

The operator sighed. "Here's what I can do. I'll take your name and number and share it with one of the officers. One of 'em should call you later just to check. I hope that helps."

Caroline provided her information to the operator, who thanked her and hung up. Not knowing what to do, she sat at the table and Rose settled in at her feet. She wasn't sure why she felt the way she did, but the numbing anxiousness in her stomach told her something wasn't right. They hadn't just gone on a walk or a drive. The car was still there, and they would have been home from a walk at this point.

Trying to calm her nerves, she got up from the table and walked to the wine cart. Noel had given it to them after the twins were born to help them "get by with two screaming babies."

She picked up a bottle of Merlot and opened it carefully as to not spill a speck on her white sweater. As she poured the wine, its rich, velvety aroma filled her nose, and the first sip warmed her throat and chest, soon calming her brain into feeling like everything was okay. And for a moment, she believed it.

Sitting back down at the table, she picked up her cellphone and hit the home button. She hoped to see a text or missed call, but only Rose's face on the home screen stared back at her, while Rose on the floor stirred slightly and let out a quick bark from the back of her throat.

* * * * *

Maria joined as the operator for the police station five weeks earlier. She answered all calls with a calm tone that never gave away her constant fear that one day something bad would happen and she'd have to be the one to hear the message and figure out what to do about it.

When she answered her most recent call, the woman's voice on the other end sounded constrained and sad because her husband and friend had been missing for a few hours. Maria didn't think much of it and asked the woman for her name, address, and telephone number for an officer to follow up.

After she hung up, she tiptoed across the office to the lunchroom where Officer McKenna was eating a tired ham sandwich. Maria called his name, and he looked up with mustard dripping down his chin.

"I'm sorry to interrupt you," she began and flipped her long, black ponytail. "But a woman named Caroline Montgomery just called and I got her information. She said that her husband and a friend suddenly disappeared a few hours ago."

"What's wrong with that?" Officer McKenna asked.

"She seemed like, um, really stressed. Like this wasn't normal. I felt really bad and told her someone would come down. I thought maybe you could. You know, just to check on her. Maybe they just went out for like a bit and didn't tell her?" said Maria.

Officer McKenna placed the sandwich down and nodded. Maria smiled. Officer McKenna was ten years her senior at thirty-five, but she liked his awkwardness and how he looked at her. She had a boyfriend, Jose, yet Officer Scott McKenna intrigued her, even with his short, full frame. He was quiet yet caring and didn't seem like a dick like some of the other cops at the station. She liked him but wasn't quite sure in what way. A friend? A brother? She didn't know yet but liked the way his dark brown eyes looked into hers and the way he tucked his brown hair under his officer's cap.

* * * * *

A few moments later, Officer McKenna passed Maria on his way to his cruiser, admiring Maria's dark skin as she talked to someone on the phone. Since she began working there, he often wondered how her skin smelled and what she looked like when she woke up in the morning.

He got in his cruiser and ventured down to the river toward Caroline's home. He knew the area well. He had been born on the other side of town but spent a lot of time near the river boating and fishing.

Pulling into the driveway, he saw a woman sitting on the front step with a dog by her side and a glass of wine in her hand. The glow from the front door light made her look young for a moment, but as Officer McKenna approached, he realized she was most likely in her late forties.

Placing the wine glass down on the step, she wiped her fingers across her face, patted the dog, and stood up, placing her hands first in her back pockets and then reached one out to Officer McKenna. He greeted her warmly, taking her extended hand.

"What seems to be the problem tonight, ma'am?" he asked, not sensing any immediate danger.

"Well, I went out to walk the dog earlier today across the street. And my husband and friend were here when I left. I came home maybe like fifteen minutes later and they weren't here," she explained with a bit of a tremble in her voice.

She explained to Officer McKenna how the back door had been left open and she noticed a scratch on the wall next to it. She also mentioned she'd talked to the neighbors. He listened and reached for this notepad.

"Do you mind if I take a look around?" he asked. She nodded and told him it was fine.

Officer McKenna entered through the front door while Caroline and Rose stayed on the front step. Frozen, smiling faces stared at him from the walls as he roamed from room to room. The house was pristine and felt cold like a museum.

In the kitchen, he noticed the scratch on the wall that Caroline mentioned. Rose trotted in as he examined the wall, with Caroline right behind her.

"Did you notice anything?" she asked, clutching the wine glass to her chest. Rose sat at her feet. He shook his head.

"Everything seems normal from what I can tell. Do you have any reason to be suspicious?" he asked. She looked blankly at him and shook her head no.

"Are you sure?" he pressed, bending down to run his fingers along the scratch. "Anyone have a grudge or an issue with either your friend or your husband?"

"No. But, I found her phone in the yard, but I haven't found my husband's," she replied and then took a breath. "I don't know what to do. I don't even know what to think. Does this happen to people normally? That was a dumb question as I suppose not."

Officer McKenna took a deep breath and began. "No. I can't say this is normal. But it is early. Only been a few hours you said?"

Caroline nodded.

He continued. "Here's what we'll do. Give it the night and then call down to the station around midday tomorrow. Maybe they just went out and called an Uber and left their phones."

Caroline swirled the wine in her glass and nodded. "Okay," she said. "I'll call down to the station tomorrow. What else should I do?"

Inching toward the door, he hoped to make his escape, but then stopped and paused. "Ma'am, I'd say nothing. I'd recommend just going to bed and see what the morning brings. I'd be interested to know where they went."

Caroline nodded again, and Officer McKenna ventured back to his car, looking forward to being back at the station to see Maria.

* * * * *

In the morning light, Caroline's eyes fluttered. For a moment, she felt that Greg was next to her. But as she turned, she was greeted by Rose's black eyes staring into hers. Normally Rose wasn't allowed on the bed, but with the sudden disappearance of both Greg and Noel, she was welcomed.

Reaching for her phone on the nightstand, she noticed that she had missed calls from both daughters who were early risers. They were always good about calling in the morning to check in before starting their day. But nothing from either Greg or Noel.

Rose hopped off the bed and Caroline heard another thump on the floor along with the four paws. Peering over the side of the bed, she saw it was Greg's phone and it was still hooked to the charger. He sometimes let it charge during the day and left it under his pillow so he wouldn't forget where it was. It was time to tell her daughters.

"Mom? Hello?" Jackie's voice rang out.

"Hold on," said Caroline. "Let me add your sister to the call."

"Hi there," Amanda then chirped.

"Are you both on?" Have either of you heard from your father?" she asked, full well knowing the answer was no.

"No, can't say that I've heard from Dad-a-rino," Amanda said.

"I haven't either," Jackie answered. "Is something wrong?"

"I don't want to upset either of you, but he and Noel seem to have gone missing," she explained.

There was silence on the other end.

"Hello?" asked Caroline. "Are you both still there?"

"Yes, Mom. We are," Jackie answered first. "Do you want me to come down? I can pick Amanda up and we can come down from the city."

"I have to work," Amanda said. "It's my afternoon to work for brunch."

"You mean you aren't going to use this as another reason to call out? What a surprise. Not like last weekend when you called out since you were hungover and lied about having the stomach bug. I'll come down," Jackie said.

CHAPTER 7

MOUNT KATAHDIN, MAINE

Sunday, May 9, at 9:30 a.m.

Marigold stood out by the dam smoking a joint and staring at the water. It was 9:30 a.m. on a Sunday. The lake was moving quickly, and the whiteheads curved at the top of the small waves.

The grandchildren were at home still sleeping. Their mother was up for the weekend with her boyfriend. They had arrived late the night before. Marigold picked up another shift at work to make extra money and get out of the house to let the grandkids spend time with their mother.

She noticed a large trash bag leaning up against a tree that abutted the dam by the lake. Odd since she hadn't noticed it the day before. Breathing in deeply, she could feel the weed going to her head. She felt relaxed and the world didn't seem so bad.

Glancing over at the trash bag again, she watched the wind flutter around it. It didn't move so she assumed it must have something heavy in it. *Rocks*, she thought, and laughed to herself.

As she puffed on her joint, she stared harder at the bag, trying to guess what it could be filled with. Imaging rocks and corn and beer bottles and baseball cards, she let her mind wander further, filling the bag with trash that no one wanted.

She decided to get up and venture over. Taking a few steps toward it, she smelled an odor. Assuming it was fish, she took a few more steps closer as the wind picked up. The odor was more intense. She stopped again, debating on whether or not she should kick the bag.

Deciding not to, she rubbed the joint out on the bottom of her shoe and started back to the inn. Guests would be checking out around 10:00 a.m., meaning she'd have several more beds to make between the lull of the early birds leaving and the later departures venturing out of Maine and back home across New England.

As she made bed after bed and pocketed tips from room to room, Marigold kept thinking about the trash bag. She debated with herself if she should remove it.

After her last room, she walked down to the kitchen where Marcus sat sipping coffee.

"You want one, too?" he asked as she plopped down.

"Yeah, I need one. My high has worn off," she replied.

Marcus shook his head and got up from the table to pour her a cup. Sitting back down, he handed it to her and smiled. "Rough morning?"

"Ugh," she started. "Same old shit. My kid's up so she's spending time with her fucking kids for once. She brought that deadbeat with her. He lays around all day except to smoke ciggies outside. I think she loves him, but there's something about him that's off. I can't figure it out. But fuck it. She'll be gone later today."

Marcus laughed. "At least she found love."

Marigold rolled her eyes. "Did you go over to the dam today?" she asked.

"No, my lady. I didn't have a chance. Been here manning the breakfast and talking to these tourists. They ain't never seen a black man in Maine. I'm giving them quite the scare," he said and laughed.

Marigold shook her head. She had always thought Marcus was handsome. His face was stern and his frame intimidating due to his height at six feet, five inches and large build. Yet, his voice and soul were kind.

"I saw this trash bag across the street and something about it just didn't seem right, you know?"

"Wanna go over and check it out?" he asked.

Marigold took a deep drink of coffee and thought about it. Something about the bag seemed off. Really off.

"Nah, man. I don't need to. Probably just some trash some asshole left not wanting it stinking up the car on the way home. Fuck it, it's fine. The DPW guys will probably come pick it up tomorrow," Marigold said.

"Don't even worry about, lady," reassured Marcus. "Some asshole leaving trash, like you said. Nothing for you to think about. Go finish cleaning up this shithole of an inn. We need to look presentable and the like to the boss."

Marigold nodded and got up from the table, placing her coffee cup in the sink.

"You better wash that, momma," Marcus chirped.

"Fuck you," she said and headed out the side door to get some air, still thinking about the bag. She made a deal with herself. If the bag was still there at 3:00 p.m. when it was time to go home, she'd go kick it.

* * * * *

Around the same time, Jackie arrived at Caroline's house, parking her white BMW sedan next to Caroline's BMW SUV. She got out and toted bagels and coffee to the door as Rose ran out to greet her.

Caroline watched Jackie walk up the path to the house. The girls weren't identical. Their only similarity was that they were the same height. Jackie looked like Greg with brown hair and green eyes yet had Caroline's thin frame and delicate features. Amanda looked like Caroline with blond hair and blue-green eyes. She was more athletic like her father in terms of build and structure. Both girls were attractive.

As Jackie entered the house, Caroline hesitated in giving her a hug and instead reached her hand out to squeeze Jackie's, unsure of how to act.

CHAPTER 8

NEWBURYPORT, MASSACHUSETTS

Caroline, Noel, and Greg, twenty-six years ago

When Caroline saw that her pregnancy test was positive, she cried. She never told anyone. The tears weren't ones of joy but of fear. This was the final sign that she was tied to Greg for the rest of her life.

Although they were married, her mind still wandered to Matt. What was he doing? Who was he with? Did he ever think of her? The practical side of her knew that if Matt was meant to be, it would have been.

She carefully folded the pregnancy test in toilet paper and stuffed it in her back pocket.

Scrubbing her hands at the sink, she looked at herself in the mirror. Greg told her that morning she was beautiful as she whipped eggs. He slapped her ass as he said it and walked away. She assumed other women would love that, but she found it disrespectful.

A few days later, she was sitting in her doctor's office waiting for the confirmed results of her test. Caroline hadn't mentioned the test to Greg or anyone. When the doctor walked in and confirmed she was pregnant, she nodded, unsure of how to act.

Noel was the first call. "That's great!" she squealed on the other end of the line. "Did you tell Greg yet, or your mother? Wow, I really can't wait to be an aunt. I'm going to smother this kid with love and stuff and let them drink underage."

Caroline laughed. "No, I haven't told Greg. Just waiting for the right time, I suppose. But can I tell you something?"

"Yes, of course you can," Noel replied.

Caroline paused. How do you even tell your closest friend that you wish the baby's father was someone else?

"I often think," she began and then stopped, not knowing how to gather the courage to make the next statement about Matt.

"I often think what? You're killing me!" Noel whined.

Caroline snapped back. "I've often thought about how I would react in this moment. And I thought it would have felt different."

"Like how?" Noel asked.

"I don't know. Just different," she replied. She agreed to tell Greg that night while Noel chatted on about all the various ways she could.

When Greg got home, dinner was on the table. She forgot the bottle of pinot noir since she wasn't going to be able to have any with the steak and carrots she had cooked. Next to the plate was an envelope containing a handwritten note with the words, "I'm pregnant" on her blue-and-white monogrammed stationery.

When Greg walked in the door, he looked tired, but his eyes lit up when he saw the meal.

"What's the occasion?" he asked.

Caroline walked over and hugged him. It was a different type of hug, the kind you give someone when you haven't seen them for months. Not the kind of hug married people give each other in their day to day.

"Wow, this has got to be really special then," he whispered in her ear. She immediately let her arms drop, feeling almost foolish and teenage-like for the display in the kitchen.

Stepping away from him, she wiped her eyes. It was time.

"Open the envelope," she requested. Looking down, he reached his hand for the envelope and opened it carefully. Halfway through opening, he leaned in and kissed her cheek.

"This better be good," he said. He slid his fingers through the rest of the seal, pulled out the paper, opened it, and blinked.

Caroline stood there and glanced at the steak. It was getting cold, she thought. She looked back at Greg who looked at her in shock.

"Are you kidding?" he asked.

She shook her head and his arms dropped to his sides, one hand now clenching the letter.

"Caroline, this is fantastic," he stated and pulled her into his arms, kissing her on the mouth and then several times on her cheek.

She felt relieved with his excitement. Greg had sometimes debated on whether or not kids would be good for them.

A few weeks later, sitting across from the doctor again with Greg at her side, they learned they were having twins. Caroline's jaw dropped. Greg laughed.

"I can't wait to do this," he said and reached for her hand, squeezing it hard.

CHAPTER 9

NEWBURYPORT, MASSACHUSETTS

*Caroline, Greg, Noel, Amanda, and Jackie,
twelve years ago*

When Amanda and Jackie were fifteen, they were busy in sports and achieving honor role. Amanda had started talking about tattoos and Jackie about Ivy League schools.

But while their differences began to show, they loved their parents equally, spending time with both. Since they were eight, Amanda had spent more time with her father, going on bike rides and fishing trips, while Jackie went shopping with her mother and enjoyed a regular manicure.

Both girls loved Noel and would clutch her hands and sit beside her at dinner when she came to visit. Noel brought the girls gifts from her worldly travels or from wherever she was living at the time.

When the girls were ten, Noel had gotten them clogs from Amsterdam and she, Caroline, and Greg watched them trip around the living room trying to dance. Amanda eventually pushed Jackie for laughing at her when she fell with the clogs on, so Caroline took both pairs away for a time when the girls would be "less tired and more focused."

"Don't be so lame," Noel had exclaimed.

"Yeah, Mom," followed Amanda. "Don't be so lame!"

Greg laughed and chimed in too. "Come on, don't be lame."

Caroline tried to hide her smile in front of the kids to hold tight to her disciplinarian status. The group then all looked at Jackie.

Feeling the pressure to participate, she sheepishly said, "Don't be lame, Mom."

The family laughed. During dinner, Noel told stories of her travels and how the airline lost her luggage once. The more she talked, the more she drank. The stories then ventured into how her boss was an asshole, and the girls laughed. Caroline resisted reminding Noel about language in front of the children.

"Bad language!" the girls both exclaimed.

She exchanged looks with Greg, who was sitting beside her, and he rubbed his foot along her leg and winked. When dinner was finished and Noel began to slur her words, he agreed to bring the kids to bed so the women could have time alone.

"I don't want to go!" cried Amanda. "I'm a woman, too, and have the right to be here!"

"Amanda, don't be dumb," said Jackie.

"Don't call your sister dumb," Greg said, ushering the girls out of the dining room. Turning back to Noel and Caroline who were sitting at the table, he mimicked putting a gun to his head with his fingers.

"So, how are you?" Noel said, all of a sudden very serious and seeming almost sober.

"I'm good," replied Caroline. "Working some and trying to get into real estate. The girls, as you can see, keep me busy. Some new neighbors moved in recently. I think they're kind of rich. They kind of look like older versions of you and Greg."

"Ugh, you're still being lame. How are you *really*? I don't care about the fucking neighbors," Noel said, holding her wine glass and leaning in.

Caroline picked up her own glass and had a long swig. She grimaced at the mouthful of pungent wine.

"Really," she began. "I'm good. Just life is life, you know? It's all about the routine and raising the girls. I write a few articles for the local paper. Things are good. It's life."

"What about Greg?" Noel inquired.

Caroline dropped her head. "I forgot about my husband," she said, then raised her head again and placed it in her hands. "Greg's good. We're in a routine. We're happy. This is our life."

Noel leaned back. "It sounds so boring. Lame."

Caroline laughed. "Well, compared to your life, it may be. But we like it and we're getting by."

"Defeatist," said Noel. "Didn't you ever want more than this? Come on, you always talked about settling down and then when Greg asked you to marry him, you jumped. You didn't even want to consider waiting it out for someone else. That was love, wasn't it? I've dated plenty of guys and haven't wanted to settle down with any of them. And look at you now, so many years in. It must be love."

Caroline never told Noel that she had doubted her relationship with Greg and the lack of passion she felt compared to Matt. She always felt so guilty since Greg had been so good to her and now, too, with raising their family.

He just came into her life so quickly after Matt left her that it helped heal the wound. Before she knew it, she was saying yes and trying to leave the idea of being with Matt behind.

Noel had always been someone who dated around and was so opened-minded about who she dated. Men and women. Caroline admired her spontaneity and openness to accept people of all kinds for who they were.

"Of course it's love," Caroline said, and took another sip of wine.

"Well, I'm dating a French guy who I met during my last time there who lives near my mom. It works out nice since I'm back and forth from New York to Paris these days," Noel said. "And in New York, I met this young college girl. She's an art student and so hot and funny."

"God, you never cease to amaze me," said Caroline.

She helped Noel to the guest bed and tucked her in an hour or so later. Noel had grabbed her hand and told her she was envious of her life before passing out. Caroline walked out of the room, shutting the light off, happy knowing she didn't have to respond.

Getting into bed with Greg, she looked him over. He was a good man. Not what she had expected, but they had a good, solid life. What else could she ask for?

The next morning, Caroline woke early to go for a run and then began making breakfast for the family. She could feel the wine remnants in her head. She realized that for the first time in a long time, she felt alive in reminiscing and living through Noel's stories of asshole bosses, love interests, and travel.

As Caroline scrambled eggs, Noel headed down the stairs, stopping in the hallway to look at pictures gracing the walls of the family and of her, Greg, and Caroline in college. She smiled as Caroline watched her look at her younger face and wild red hair that had since been cut. Caroline then focused back on the eggs.

Greg came down shortly behind Noel. "Good morning."

"Good morning," Noel replied. Pointing to one photo on the wall, she said, "Look at this one and how young and happy we looked at graduation."

Greg stood next to her and leaned in to look. "That's a good picture," he remarked.

Noel nodded and smiled. It was of the three of them. Caroline was standing slightly away, while Greg and Noel had their arms around each other.

"Do you remember how we tried to get Caroline to drink all night with us that night to celebrate, and how she couldn't and fell asleep by 10:30 p.m.?" he said.

Noel laughed again. "I do remember that. God, what a hangover I had that day. I hated you and the world. I was so fucking sick."

As they laughed, Amanda popped out of her room and ran down the hall and around the corner, excited to see her aunt Noel. She stopped short when she reached the top of the stairs as she saw her father's hand run down the length of Noel's back.

Amanda stood quietly and watched her father look down at Noel. Noel looked up at him. He was looking at her the way he sometimes looked at her mother after too much wine.

At that same moment, Jackie screamed from her room about a spider, and Noel and Greg both looked up toward the noise, seeing Amanda standing there silently.

The two looked startled, and Noel scurried toward the kitchen and Greg up the stairs. He passed Amanda without saying a word and ventured toward Jackie's room to address the spider issue.

No one ever breathed a word about the interrupted moment again.

CHAPTER 10

MOUNT KATAHDIN, MAINE

Sunday, May 9, at 4:05 p.m.

The day was winding down for Marigold, but the trash bag was still stuck in her head. Standing outside in the driveway of the inn, she could see its shape on the horizon. She took a deep drag of her cigarette and debated walking over to it.

Looking to her left, she saw a car coming up the road toward her and the looming mountain beyond. So many tourists drove by each day. She was always surprised that so many people from around the country, even around the world, would venture this far into Maine to see some mountain.

The car passed and she breathed out the fumes. She took one step, then another, crossing the road, and getting closer and closer until she was in the dirt parking lot. The bag was closer now. It looked like one of those carpenter's trash bags, the big, heavy kind that was used to haul junk away after a construction project. The same type of bag Sammy always had in his truck.

Standing there facing the bag, she felt a moment of fear, and questions raced through her mind. When did the bag get there? She hadn't noticed it yesterday. What if there was a dead animal in it that someone was trying to get rid of? Like a skunk or a raccoon?

Who left the bag? A tourist? A local? A passerby? She took another deep puff of her cigarette. What if it was just filled with someone's shit like she had thought before? Like soup cans, empty beer bottles, or spoiled food?

She took another few steps toward the bag. It seemed even larger now. And there was even more of a smell. The smell reminded her of roadkill on Route 95 on a muggy August night. Marigold flicked her cigarette to the side.

She opened her mouth. "Dear God, I know we don't talk much, but give me the strength to do this." She blessed herself, pulled her long hair back, and took another few steps forward.

Now the bag was about five feet in front of her. She pulled her T-shirt up over her nose, scared she would get another faint whiff. The muddled shape was too large to be an animal or someone's bag of leftover stuff.

Next to where her cigarette was smoldering was a stick. Marigold dug the toe of her cowboy boot into the cigarette and reached for the stick, not once taking her eyes off the bag. Picking the stick up and bringing it close to her face, she looked at one end and then the other.

One end was sharp, the other end duller. It was almost as tall as she was. Sliding the dull part into her hand, she reached the sharper point out toward the bag and then stopped.

"What the fuck am I doing?" she said out loud and then looked around to see if anyone heard her or was watching this strange scene. Looking to the sky, she took another breath.

Taking one more deep breath, she jabbed the bag softly with the stick. It felt soft, yet hard. She pulled back and took another breath, tasting the tobacco on her tongue.

"That's it," she said and pulled the stick back then quickly plunged it forward into the bag.

It still had a hard and soft feeling that made her think of a dead pig. She knew that feeling from her childhood when her mother's boyfriend would slaughter one of his pigs and throw it in the back of his truck to take to his butcher friend to help him chop it up.

One day, her brother dared her to touch the pig. She was scared but wanted to show him she was tough. He called her a chicken and a pussy and threw a stick at her. Marigold picked up the stick, similarly to what she was doing today. And similar to that day, she poked the dead pig in the back of the truck. It felt the same as this.

Remembering that moment, she felt sick, but she reminded herself of who she was, and she was a tough chick. She was scared then and got over it and she was scared now. Marigold was going to get over this, too.

She gave the bag another sharp and quick jab so that it tore a hole in the thick, black skin of the trash bag. She smelled another faint odor. Kneeling down and dropping the stick, she reached out her hand toward the small hole in the bag.

Wiggling one finger in, she made a bigger hole. Reaching her other hand over, she began to spread the torn pieces of the bag apart. Leaning over it, she tried to get a better look inside. It didn't seem like it was trash, and there was no skunk smell.

Leaning over the bag, she moved back and forth trying to catch the dimming Maine sunlight in a way that would help her see into it. She finally got a glimpse and immediately fell back, pushing herself away with her feet across the ground.

Gasping for air, she blinked. Did she just see what she thought she did? Pulling herself up to her knees, she crawled back toward the bag. Moving around the bag again, she tried to catch the light and her breath. She realized she was right.

It was the bright-orange-painted fingernail of a woman's hand.

"This has got to be a fucking joke," she said out loud. Still moving around the small hole to examine her findings, she wondered if it could be a mannequin. But remembering the feeling of pushing the stick into the pig, she knew it wasn't.

"Yo, Marigold! What you got going on over there?"

She turned to look. It was Marcus.

"Marcus, don't come over here! Call the cops!" she screamed back. He stood there looking at her in disbelief. "Jesus, are you deaf? Go call the fucking cops. I think this is a dead body."

Marcus flushed and ran back toward the inn. Marigold flipped from all fours to sitting on her butt. Reaching for her cigarettes, she pulled one out, lit it up, and took a long, deep inhale.

"This is some fucked up shit," she said and dropped her head.

CHAPTER 11

NEWBURYPORT, MASSACHUSETTS

Sunday, May 9, at 11:17 a.m.

"**D**id you call the police?" Jackie asked and then took a sip of her latte.

"Yes, and a nice man came over, but he said to wait until this morning to call back. I wanted you and your sister to know first. I guess I should call now. What do you think?" Caroline asked.

Jackie sighed and picked up her phone. "Yeah, I guess you should. Do you have any idea about what could have happened? I texted and called them both."

"Their phones are here. Frank noticed hers in the yard and your father's was upstairs under his pillow. It would make no difference if you called or texted," Caroline replied. "Dad never leaves his phone. Noel is always losing hers and ignoring calls and texts."

"What could have happened to them?" Jackie asked.

"I just don't know. I was up most of the night thinking about this. Do you think it could be some sort of joke or a surprise? I mean, who just disappears like that? I was right across the way with Rose," said Caroline.

Jackie cleared the latte residue from her throat. "Do you think I should call Dad and Noel again?"

Caroline reached for her own phone from the counter. Scrolling through her call history, it seemed so strange to her that her last call was to the girls, the call before that to the police, and the calls before that bounced between Greg and Noel. And now she couldn't get ahold of either one of them. It was surreal.

She pressed the police number again and took a breath. Jackie listened to both the faint voice of the woman on the other end and the quivering voice of her mother.

"Hello, yes, I called last night," Caroline began. "Officer McKenna came to my home. I called because my friend and husband were missing."

Maria, who had picked up the line, remembered Caroline's voice and how strange it sounded that her husband and friend would go missing like that.

"Yes, ma'am, I remember," Maria answered. Jackie leaned across the counter to hear more. "Are they back yet?"

Jackie shook her head as if she were answering.

"No, they aren't, I fear," Caroline answered. "I don't even know what to do next. Should you contact Officer McKenna? Is there anyone else who I should speak to?"

"I'm sorry ma'am. It hasn't been twenty-four hours and Officer McKenna is undisposed at the moment," Maria answered.

Jackie and Caroline rolled their eyes at each other for a moment, forgetting about why they were even calling in the first place.

"Indisposed?" Caroline asked. Jackie covered her mouth.

"He's out right now," she answered, not realizing her mistake.

"Is there anyone else I can talk to?" Caroline pressed. Jackie began waving her hands around, frustrated by the lack of effort on the other end. Caroline got up and walked away from her distracting daughter.

"Ma'am, I can have someone call you later. Would that be okay?" she asked.

Caroline nodded. "Yes," she finally said. "That would be fine."

Hanging up, she turned back to Jackie, who looked annoyed.

"Mom, what the hell? Why were you so soft on them?" she demanded.

"Jackie, what do you want me to do? Go down there?" replied Caroline.

"Yeah, do something," Jackie retorted. "You're always so passive and cold. Like, this is screwed up. Where is Dad? Where is Noel? Are you not telling me something? Is this a fucking joke? What is going on here?"

At that moment, Caroline wished she was alone. Rose walked into the kitchen and sat at her feet as if she sensed that Caroline needed her. Bending over, she patted Rose's head. "Who's a good girl? My girl?" Rose looked up at her, matching her gaze.

"Jackie, I wish I knew. I really wish I did, but I told you. We were here hanging out. I took Rose across the street for a few minutes to swim in the river and when I came back, they were gone. I don't know what else to say. I'm at a loss myself," Caroline answered.

Jackie placed her head in her hands and said, "Mom, I'm sorry. I am. I'm just freaking out. I mean, how do you think I feel? My dad and aunt are missing and my mom is acting helpless."

Caroline walked across the kitchen. Standing behind Jackie, she wished that Greg was there. He was always so calm in moments like this. If Noel had been missing, Greg would have known what to do and would have taken charge, quietly finding a solution.

If it had been Greg who was missing, Noel would have been like Jackie, demanding an answer. Noel would have been running around and in the car driving around, banging on the door at the police station, and screaming at the girl who answered the phone.

But neither one was there. Caroline looked out the window at the neighbors who were milling around their yard. Jackie was back on her phone. Rose leaned against Caroline's leg just as it began to shake.

CHAPTER 12

UNIVERSITY OF MASSACHUSETTS, AMHERST, MASSACHUSETTS

Caroline and Noel, thirty-two years ago

On a Sunday afternoon in mid-May, Noel and Caroline sat on the porch of the house where Noel was renting an apartment. The day was overly sunny and hot for the Berkshires. Noel was swinging side to side on the porch swing with one leg dangling down. She had a joint in one hand and a beer in the other.

Caroline was laying on the deck face up staring at the peeling paint on the porch ceiling. She had finally stopped crying and took a few hits off Noel's joint.

Noel, with joint back in hand, took a puff, held her breath, and then let the smoke out her nose. "Fuck him," she said.

Caroline looked over. She was talking about Matt. He stood her up the night before, leaving her confused and angry. Yet, she had no more tears to cry. He'd been doing that all the time lately.

"Why would he do that?" Caroline asked, turning her head to Noel who brought the joint again to her lips.

Eyeing it and flicking off the ash, she focused back on Caroline. "Because he's a fucking asshole. That's why. Men who are cowards do that shit. Men who are ball-less do that shit." She paused and took another puff.

Breathing out, she began again. "Men who have no respect for women do that shit. Caroline, you need to get over this dude. I know I sound like some cliché being like, 'girl, find another guy' but, legit. Girl, find another guy."

Caroline turned her gaze back to the ceiling. Closing her eyes, she imagined Matt standing in front of her and what she'd say to him. A bubble began to form again in her chest, rising up through her throat, signaling that more tears were about to come.

"Noel, I just really like him. I really do, and I want him to be in my life," Caroline said and then stopped, feeling silly about being so expressive and fearful of what she'd say next.

Noel looked down at her friend, took a sip of beer, and said, "What else were you going to say?"

Caroline turned away and looked back at the ceiling. Noel always did this. She always knew when Caroline was holding back, or so she thought. Taking a breath, she turned back to Noel.

"Can I have another hit off that?" Caroline asked, pulling herself up.

Noel nodded and handed the joint to her. Caroline brought it to her lips, taking a big inhale, and then coughed. She handed it back to Noel, who did the same minus the cough.

"I think he's the one. Like, the man I can see myself marrying and having a family with. Like, I can just picture us so clearly now and in the future," Caroline said then looked down again, feeling vulnerable for such a soulful statement.

Noel used her foot to stop herself from rocking and pulled herself from the swing and down onto the floor facing Caroline. She handed her the beer. Caroline took a big sip, emptying the can.

"We have our whole fucking lives ahead of us," Noel said. "He's just one dude. Not the only dude. Is he really worth getting this worked up about? Plus, this is like the final week of school of our junior year. Don't you have other stuff to focus on with like grades and shit?"

Desperately wanting to change the subject, Caroline nodded. "I have a final article to write for my journalism class and a few other finals to study for. You're right. I should put him out of my mind."

Noel nodded and took another hit off the joint. "I think I'm in love with a woman."

"Oh!" Caroline cried out. It wouldn't be the first time that Noel had used the L word, and it wouldn't be the first time that she was into a woman. But it was the first time that both were used in the same sentence.

"Who is she? Do I know her?" Caroline asked.

Licking the tips of her fingers, Noel rubbed the tip of the joint out, placing it gently on the porch floor.

"I met her in one of my art history classes. Her name is Loyola and she's super cute. I met up with her last night. We made out for a few hours. I really like her. We're going out again on Thursday," said Noel.

"We'll see," Caroline said. "But I'm glad you met someone. Are you going to make plans with her this summer to hang out?"

"It's too early to tell," said Noel.

Caroline laughed.

"What's so funny?" Noel asked.

"Noel, you just said you loved her but don't know if you want to hang out with her this summer? That's so weird," Caroline responded.

"I mean like love in a general sense. Like, I just love her vibe. I'm not saying that I met my soulmate like you," Noel said.

With that, Caroline's heart sank again remembering that Matt was going back home to California for the summer in a few weeks and she was headed to the Cape.

Realizing her mistake, Noel reached her hand across to Caroline's. Looking her in the eyes, she smiled and squeezed Caroline's cold hand.

"Hey, I didn't mean it like that. I just think with Matt you could do better, okay?"

Caroline nodded. She knew that Noel meant well, and she knew that Noel was right. But she hoped that when she got home, there'd be a note on her door from him or a voicemail on her answering machine.

Noel squeezed Caroline's hand again, bringing her back to the moment. "You can do better," she said again and smiled.

CHAPTER 13

MOUNT KATAHDIN, MAINE

Sunday, May 9, at 4:23 p.m.

Officer Tommy Kelly grew up in southern Maine. He was over six feet tall and well-built, with knowing brown eyes and brown hair that he kept tucked neatly under his peaked cap. He studied criminal justice at a state university and began working in Millinocket a few years after graduating. He liked being so close to the mountain because he was an active guy. When he pulled tourists over, they'd often remark at how handsome he was.

Between shifts at the station, he worked as a whitewater rafting guide by the inn. He had met a nice girl, Emma, from Portland, who drove up every few weeks to see him. She was tall and thin with long brown hair and brown eyes. Emma had the "girl next door" look and was a few years younger than him at twenty-seven. He had just turned thirty. The two looked perfect together.

Emma was teaching fifth grade and was unsure if that far up in Maine was right for her. But Tommy hoped that her weekends there with him would change her mind. He liked the way she looked in the morning when he woke up and she lay beside him snoring ever so lightly with her feathery eyelashes fluttering every few seconds.

In those moments, he wanted to take a picture, but knew she'd be creeped out by that. Instead, he'd just stare at her and smell her skin. When she finally started to wake up, he'd lay back, propping his head on the pillow.

"Good morning, gorgeous," he always said, and she'd laugh, pawing one hand out to lay on his chest, right where his tattoo of a bulldog wearing a police hat was located.

She wasn't around this weekend, so Officer Kelly spent it hanging around the station. When the call came in around 4:00 p.m., he picked it up figuring it was some lost tourist looking for directions back to the highway, or some local drunk calling about a raccoon.

"Good even—" he started to say, then looked at this watch and stopped, realizing it wasn't quite time to say that. "Good afternoon, East Millinocket police station. Officer Kelly here. How can I help?"

"Hell, hell, hello?" the voice fumbled. Officer Kelly assumed this was going to be a joke.

"Uh, yes, how can I help you?" he asked. "Is there a problem?"

"Hi, this is Marcus up at the inn," he said softly but nervously. "We need someone to get up here and quick."

Assuming it was an issue with a tourist, he leaned back in his chair. Marcus had called a few times over the last few months with minor issues like someone not wanting to settle up their bill, or a guest getting a bit too drunk and rude.

"Marcus, can you tell me more about the issue?" he asked. "I can come up but I want to know what I'm getting myself into."

Silence on the other end.

"Marcus, are you there?" Officer Kelly asked, now leaning closer to the table.

"Officer Kelly, we got a real problem up here. I think we, or really Marigold found a body. Now, I'm not an expert, so maybe this is a doll or some sort of mannequin or shit, I sure do hope so, but we think it's a body," Marcus said.

Officer Kelly stood up stunned at what he heard. "A body?" he asked. "Are you sure? Marcus, man, is this some type of joke?"

"It's no joke. I hope to hell I'm wrong," said Marcus. "But Marigold saw some trash bag out by the pond near the dam and had her eye on it all day. She went out there now and opened it and saw something and said it was a body. Can you come on up here? We're too scared to check."

"Yes, I'm on my way," Officer Kelly said, dropping the phone. "Brenda, I'm going up to the inn. They say they may have a body up there."

Brenda looked up, expressionless. She was the normal dispatcher but had been out back having a snack. She had heard a lot during her twenty-plus years of working in the town in various roles, but not this.

"A body?" she asked and removed her glasses.

Officer Kelly nodded. During his time on the force, he had gotten calls to help injured people off the mountain, but that had only happened a few times. A body was something he had never encountered and figured it was some sort of sick joke or misunderstanding.

Getting into his car, he put the siren on and began the journey up the road. His mind danced from thought to thought. Considering if this was a dead body and not some joke, what was he going to do?

Or, worse yet, if this was a joke, how could he justify locking Marcus up for the night to punish him for screwing with his head like this? Marcus and some of the others weren't always friends to Officer Kelly and the others on the force, so maybe this was a chance to get him back, something he could tell Emma about when he called her later that night. He wanted to tell her about a deer he saw earlier that day. Emma loved deer, and he always wanted to tell her about the little things that he saw that would make her happy.

Pulling up to the dam parking lot, he saw Marcus and a few others hovering over Marigold, who was sitting there smoking and rocking back and forth. Marigold was tough, but this didn't look like her. This looked like a scared child and not a short woman with a big attitude.

Marcus looked up and waved at Officer Kelly. He took a deep breath when he realized this wasn't a joke. He opened the car door and began walking up the small hill to where the group huddled around Marigold and her cloud of smoke.

"Marigold, you want to tell me what happened here?" Officer Kelly asked. "Are you all playing some type of joke?"

Marigold lifted her head to look up at him and motioned past the small crowd. Officer Kelly looked in the direction she was pointing and saw a large, black plastic bag.

"We think there's a body in there, sir," she said and shook her head. "A body."

Officer Kelly looked at Marcus, who nodded.

"Did you see a body?" Officer Kelly asked, surprised she was calling him sir. He saw her at a local bar often and she was always telling him a joke or a funny story about a guest at the inn.

"No, sir," answered Marcus. "From what Marigold said, there's no way I'm going over there. That's why we called you. She said she saw a lady's finger through that hole."

Officer Kelly knew he had to go over to the bag but felt a stream of fear flood his body. Not wanting to have an audience in case he threw up or was painted to be a fool if this actually turned out to be a well-played joke, he asked the crowd to move back across the street to the inn.

Marcus reached down to try to help Marigold up.

"Stay right there," Officer Kelly instructed. He didn't want Marigold or Marcus going anywhere. If this turned out to be a joke, he wanted them within arm's reach to handcuff them. Marcus froze and nodded, surprised by the sternness of the normally laid-back officer.

Officer Kelly began walking toward the bag. His heart was beating fast and hard, but he wanted to look like a real cop so he didn't show any signs of fear. He knew people didn't take him seriously and saw him as the "fun" cop. With Marigold and Marcus behind him, he picked up his radio.

"Brenda, you there?" he whispered, still wanting to put on a strong persona for the crowd in the background.

"Yeah, I'm here," she answered. "What's going on up there? Still think this is some kind of joke?"

"No, I don't think it is. I'm going to check out this rather large bag up here, so I'll radio back in a few. I hope this turns out to be nothing," he said.

"Me too," she answered as Officer Kelly arrived at the bag.

Looking down, he saw a stick and a small hole in the side. Bending down on one knee, he picked the stick up and tossed it aside. Breathing in, he smelled something foul like rotting meat left uncooked from a barbeque.

Looking at the hole and bending closer, he couldn't quite tell. Reaching into his pocket, he pulled out a pair of rubber gloves that he'd stuck in there earlier that day. Putting them over his hands, he reached down, sliding the index finger of his right hand into the hole.

Bringing his left hand to the bag, he slid his left finger in to widen the hole. At first, he saw something white. Then he pulled harder, widening the hole to see a hand with a few large and colorful rings on the fingers and orange polish on the nails.

This has to be a doll, he thought, and pulled more. Opening the hole wider and wider, the way a child opens a gift on Christmas, the hand led to an arm with a black sleeve. Officer Kelly put his other knee to the ground and pulled the bag open with both of his hands.

When he looked down, he fell back realizing what he saw. It was the torso of a woman. Her skin was white and her hair was red and curly. It was so dark inside, it was hard for him to tell where the hair ended and the bag began.

Pulling the bag down further around her waist, he gained his first glimpse of blood. It was pooling at the bottom of the bag like she had been placed in waist down with her head at the top of the bag.

Awestruck with what he was seeing, Officer Kelly kneeled again next to the woman and placed his fingers on her neck to check for a pulse and immediately felt stupid.

Taking off one glove and then the other, he took a deep breath. The only way he was going to know for sure if this was a doll or not was to touch her skin. He knew he'd know for sure just by touching her.

When his grandfather died a few years ago, he touched his hand in the casket. It was cold and unlike anything he had ever felt before. He committed that feeling to memory and knew that if he ever felt it again, he'd know that was the feeling of death and nothing more.

Moving his hands slowly down, his skin met the skin of the woman's arm. First his right hand and then his left. He paused and took a breath then pulled his hands quickly back as if he had been burned. He pulled for his radio again.

Hitting the button, he paused to take a breath, then said, "Brenda, are you there?"

Brenda answered right away. "Tommy," she said in a hushed voice. "What's going on up there? Is this a joke, or is it really a body?"

"It's a body," he answered. "And something really bad has happened to her. Can you call the hospital and call the county sheriff? Call whoever you can."

"Okay, Tommy, I will," Brenda answered. Officer Kelly put down the radio and blessed himself quickly, hoping that the people behind him wouldn't see. He got up and began walking back to them to clear the area.

Marcus and Marigold looked up from their cigarettes and watched him walk closer. They looked hopeful for a moment, thinking that maybe it was a misunderstanding. Officer Kelly shook his head no ever so slightly and their faces changed back to being scared.

"I'm going to need you both to sit over by the cruiser. Don't go anywhere as we're going to have to have a conversation," he said and kept walking across the street toward the inn to shoo away the crowd.

As he crossed and began waving people away, he heard the faint cry of the ambulance from down the road. He couldn't wait to tell Emma. She was never going to believe this.

CHAPTER 14

NORTHAMPTON, MASSACHUSETTS

Caroline and Greg, thirty-two years ago

On a rainy November night during their senior year, Greg met Caroline at a local pizza place. He was planning to pick her up, but he was coming right from his job as a file clerk for a local financial advisor. Caroline was coming from class but had stopped by Noel's house to make sure she looked okay.

She wasn't overly excited for the date and had run into Matt a few times over the previous weeks. She pictured Matt's face constantly and thought she saw him everywhere.

Noel really liked Greg and thought he and Caroline would click. Caroline had met him a few times, but nothing about him stood out to her the way that everything about Matt did.

She sat in a booth with a cheery red-and-white-checkered tablecloth. The girl behind the counter walked over and asked if she wanted a beer. She said yes even though it was a weeknight.

Greg came through the door after she was a few sips into her beer. Rushing to the table, he apologized and reached his wet hand to hers. The two fumbled, as she tried to avoid his wet hand and he tried to scoop her entire hand up with his.

"Jesus, I'm really sorry about this," he said and sat down, forgetting to take his coat off. He looked at her and realized what he had done.

"Oh shit, I should take this off or I'm going to be sitting in a puddle all night," he said and began pulling his coat off while maintaining eye contact with her. "Have you been waiting very long?"

With his coat off, he reached up to push his glasses back onto the bridge of his nose. Caroline didn't remember him being this clumsy and unkempt or talkative even, but she smiled and told him it had only been a few minutes.

"Oh great. That's not bad then," he said and looked around the place. The girl at the counter had noticed his arrival and walked over to take their order.

"Can I get a beer?" asked Greg and then looked at Caroline. "You want to get a pizza?"

"Yes, that'd be great," she said and fumbled for the one menu in the middle of the table, surprised by how quickly he wanted to order.

The girl seemed to sense the first-date tension. "Why don't I give you both a minute to look at the menu while I get that beer," she said with a smile and walked behind the counter.

With Matt, this was easy. They both liked cheese and got it every time. No added salt or pepper flakes or fancy toppings. Glancing at the menu, she felt the same as she always had. She wanted cheese.

Pushing the menu across the table, she told Greg she didn't care what they got. It was a lie. She did care but didn't want to tell him.

"They make a great pepper pizza here," he said.

She winced. Peppers were one of her least favorite foods. Greg noticed the strain in her face.

"You don't like peppers?" he asked. She shook her head.

"Okay then, no peppers," he said and looked back at the menu.

"Why don't you pick?" he said as the waitress came back over to hand off his beer.

Caroline looked at her and said, "One large cheese pizza, please."

"You got it," said the waitress and walked away.

Greg smiled. "Cheese is good," he said. "It's stable, trusting. I like it."

Caroline smiled. He was kind of charming and his green eyes twinkled under the cheap pizza place lights.

"Tell me more about you," he said. "What are you into? I like lacrosse and running. Plus, golf and Chinese food. I spend time with my family in Rhode Island and Connecticut."

Caroline paused. She wasn't quite sure how to answer but began telling him about her love of journalism and friendship with Noel. He nodded throughout.

After a bit, the waitress came by to drop off the pizza. Greg reached for a piece and took a bite but dropped it quickly.

"Too hot," he said and reached for his beer. Caroline giggled, although she was surprised that he would have done something so dumb.

"You need to wait a few," she advised. "Tell me more about you."

Greg told her about his family and his friends and his love of the outdoors and biology. He told her about how he wanted to work in finance after college and move to the North Shore.

They ordered another round of beers. Greg paid and left the waitress a five-dollar tip. She waved to them as they left and winked at Caroline. Greg put his hand on the small of her back and walked her to her car. He hugged her but didn't try for a kiss.

In the embrace, he told her that he had a great time and wanted to see her again. Pulling back, she looked at him and smiled. Nodding her head, she agreed.

In the car, she took a deep breath. For the first time in months, she hadn't thought about Matt for hours and realized that her time with Greg hadn't been so bad. He was kind and she liked that.

CHAPTER 15

NEWBURYPORT, MASSACHUSETTS

Sunday, May 9, at 3:11 p.m.

Jackie decided she would drive the pair to the police station. Caroline took the passenger seat. Jackie turned the car on and a Lady Gaga song played loudly. She quickly reached over to lower the music. When they arrived at the station, Caroline opened the door and slowly put one foot and then the other onto the sidewalk.

"Mom, should I come too?" Jackie asked.

"No, I'll go alone," she replied. She didn't want Jackie screaming at her in the police station and still hadn't figured out what she was going to say. She closed the car door and began walking toward the door to the station.

Pulling open the door, she saw a pretty, young girl sitting behind the thick glass. Behind her was a wall plastered with pictures of criminals and phone numbers for services and help. To the side was an open door that led to where the police sat.

Maria looked up and said hello through the microphone. Caroline smiled and pushed her blond hair back.

"Hi there," she began. "I called earlier. My husband and friend are missing. Officer McKenna came by my house last night."

Maria nodded. "Yes ma'am. I remember."

Caroline felt a twinge of frustration that her answer wasn't more helpful or empathetic.

"They still aren't back yet. It's been over twenty-four hours. Now what do I do?" Caroline inquired.

Maria looked at her, expressionless. Caroline raised her eyebrows and put her head forward to indicate that she wanted an answer.

Maria took the subtle hint. "I'll find Officer McKenna," she answered and got up from the desk, moving through the doorway and out of sight.

"Fucking idiot," Caroline said softly to herself, almost channeling Noel's way of speaking.

Officer McKenna appeared, followed by Maria. Bending over, he put his mouth to the microphone.

"Hello again," he said. "Still no sign?"

"Can you come out here and talk to me face-to-face?" Caroline said, crossing her arms. He nodded and moved to the door.

"Still no sign?" he asked again as he approached her.

She shook her head. "No. And, both of their phones are here. What happens next?" she asked.

"I can let the other officers know," Officer McKenna said. "I can do a drive around if you send their photos, so I know who I'm looking for. I'm hope for your sake they still show up. Maybe it's some sort of misunderstanding still. There's not much else I can do."

As he finished, Jackie came flying through the door, first looking at her mother, then at Maria, and then at Officer McKenna.

"What's going on? What are you all doing to find my dad and my aunt?" she demanded.

Officer McKenna told her the same thing he told Caroline. Jackie shook her head.

"That's all you can do? Can't you do like an ADP or something?" she asked.

Officer McKenna smirked. "I can do a BOLO, but they are adults. They have freedoms to come and go when they want to or need to. We're doing all we can."

Caroline wanted to leave. It was clear these two people were going to be of no help. And maybe he was right, that there was nothing else that could be done, and it was just a matter of waiting for them to show up again.

"Jackie, I think that's all they can do right now," Caroline said. "Let's go home and call your sister to come up. Thank you both."

"But, Mom," Jackie whined.

"Time to go. Thank you both," Caroline said and headed to the door with Jackie behind her.

In the car, Jackie called her sister, telling her to come up. Caroline opened the window. She debated whether she should call Tom at the newspaper and see if he could post an article or something. She also debated to herself about posting something on social media but feared the embarrassment. What if Noel and Greg ran off together and this was just bound to happen? Or maybe it was worse.

Either way, she was too prideful and unsure to do anything just yet and decided to give it one more night. Maybe on Monday when the week started, they'd come back to their senses about work and reality and come home with an explanation.

"Amanda is on her way," Jackie said, starting the car and pulling out of the parking lot.

Back in the station, Maria and Officer McKenna were talking about Caroline and the situation.

"God, I hope they show up," Maria said. "I feel so bad but don't know what else to say."

Officer McKenna nodded. "I can't imagine what would have happened to them. Seems so odd for them to just disappear like that. When I was out at the house last night, everything seemed fine. It was just her and the dog. How could two people just disappear like that? Unless they were having an affair or something and ran off together?"

Maria nodded her head, agreeing with his point. "This is just stunning," she said. "Absolutely stunning."

"Yeah, it is," he replied. "But I also have more stuff to do than worry about this shit."

CHAPTER 16

MOUNT KATAHDIN, MAINE

Sunday, May 9, at 4:41 p.m.

Chong Wen loved biking. He was thin yet muscular from his passion for cycling. He drove to Maine every year in May to pedal along the quiet roads. He was a lawyer in Albany and worked at least eighty hours a week. Every few months, he'd drive from New York to various parts within the state to bike, but he liked Baxter State Park the most.

Pedaling from the mountain down Golden Road, beads of sweat dripped from under his helmet down his face. He could also hear sirens ahead of him.

Chong was a quiet guy and more empathetic than your typical lawyer. He needed the time away to clear his head and reflect on why he chose to become a lawyer. It was to help people, but sometimes all the money and fighting made him lose focus on his life's true purpose.

Pedaling faster, the noise of the sirens was closer now. Chong's heart flipped. Pulling the brake forward on the bike, he slowed down and started to pull over to the side of the road. Once stopped, he pulled a granola bar out of his bike pack and the water bottle from its basket and ventured into a patch of tall grass. He took a drink and looked from one side to another. Once again, he was blown away by the beauty of Maine.

Lying back, he stared up at the clouds. It was about 4:25 p.m. and he started to plan the rest of the day. He'd finish his ride in a few minutes, take a nap, and try to venture out for some dinner and a Maine beer. He wanted to turn in early since tomorrow he'd head back to Albany early in the morning.

He liked doing that, although it made for a long day, leaving the inn at 4:00 a.m. and getting to his office around 11:00 a.m. If he was lucky, he would work the rest of the day there and some evening hours at home. But he still had plenty of time before the day was over, and he was determined to enjoy every minute of it.

A cloud floated by. Chong thought about how cliché it was for him to be staring at clouds. Here he was a top lawyer, single and attractive, lying in a field in Maine next to a dirt road staring at the sky.

Rolling to his side, he looked up toward some trees. Behind one, he saw a flash of red. He sat up and looked around, almost forgetting about the sirens he'd heard below near his destination.

Standing up, he peered over, wondering who would have dumped trash behind a tree out here in pure paradise. *How inconsiderate*, he thought, and moved toward the tree to pick up whatever had been discarded. He didn't have much further to go and felt that picking up trash was the right thing to do, so he'd consider it his good deed for that day, decluttering the natural beauty.

As Chong walked toward the trees, he smelled a faint smell of something like a dead animal. Walking closer, the red glimmer became larger and larger, and there was something else off to the side. It looked like a white, oddly shaped board.

Getting closer, Chong stopped. He looked around, trying to comprehend what he saw. Behind the tree, a man was lying on the ground staring up at him. He wore a red polo shirt and dark jeans. His shoes were gone.

Looking to the right, he realized the board wasn't a board at all. It was the bottom half of a person. Chong felt his stomach shake and the granola bar he had eaten move from his stomach and out of his mouth. His hand reached for the tree that the man lay behind and he turned to the side, throwing up. Dizzy with confusion and disgust, it occurred to him that maybe the sirens had something to do with this.

But the terror of the sight was too much. Falling to the ground, he knew he had to get up and get help. But what could help do? It was obviously too late for these people. Pulling his bike up, he began to walk toward the sound of the sirens. His walk became a run and he started to say, "Help."

At first, his cry for help was a whisper. He began to get louder, then faster. He was running now and screaming as he approached the police cars, ambulance, and a small crowd of people.

"Help!" he cried and waved his free arm while the other guided the bike. "Help, dear God! Please!"

An officer began running toward him, and Chong stopped in an attempt to catch his breath.

"Sir, are you okay?" the officer asked. It was Officer Kelly.

"No, no, man, I'm not," cried Chong, falling to the ground alongside his bike. He began waving his arm pointing back in the direction from which he came. "There's a body. There's a body and like half a person."

"What? Legs? Another body?" Officer Kelly asked, feeling sick again. *How could there be legs?* he thought, and then realized this half must belong to the woman.

"Please," Chong whimpered, still trying to catch his breath. "Please go look. Please go look and tell me that I'm wrong."

Officer Kelly knew that the man wasn't wrong, and at the same moment, it clicked in Chong's mind that the other half of the body was here. He threw up again, and at that moment vowed he would never visit there again.

CHAPTER 17

NEWBURYPORT, MASSACHUSETTS

Sunday, May 9, at 5:23 p.m.

The sleepiness of a late Sunday afternoon crawled in as Amanda pulled into the driveway of her mother's house, her long blond ponytail flapping in the breeze from the open window. She was optimistic that by the time she arrived, her father and Noel would be there, and Jackie and her mother would have finally calmed down.

Jackie always had been high strung. Her father, not so much, and her mother would go back and forth. Amanda felt that she had gotten her easygoing nature from her father.

Growing up, Amanda had traveled with Noel and knew about the stories Noel didn't want Caroline to know, like the pink-and-blue butterfly tattoo she added to her back a few months ago and the threesome she had in Italy.

Jackie didn't want to be bothered with Noel now as an adult. Sure, the two of them hugged at Christmas and texted on birthdays, but they didn't connect the way that Noel and Amanda did or the odd way that Caroline and Noel did.

Amanda thought back to that day so long ago when she noticed her father's hand grazing Noel's back. Although she and Noel were close, she never brought it up, and neither did Noel.

It crossed her mind that maybe Noel and her father had been in love all this time and finally decided to run off together.

She knew it would ruin their relationship with Caroline and, potentially, her and Jackie.

Parking her car next to her sister's, Amanda got out and walked to the side door that led to the screened-in porch where her mother and sister sat. It seemed eerily quiet, and the two seemed undisturbed by her entrance as they sipped white wine.

"Uh, hi?" Amanda said. The two looked at her.

"Hi," they replied in unison.

"What's going on?" Amanda asked, trying to gauge what was happening.

Jackie began. "Fucking nothing. These local town cops are useless. We've called and gone down there. There's nothing they can do. And Mom is being super weird about this whole thing."

"Jackie, I'm right here," Caroline snapped. She looked at Amanda and shook her head. "They are hesitant about doing anything. It hasn't been long enough, and they are grown adults, so we have to wait."

"This is so crazy," Jackie said, and took a gulp of her wine.

"Okay, let me drop my bag and get a drink," Amanda said and walked toward the screen door leading into the house.

Walking through the door, Amanda looked to her right and saw the scratch that Caroline had first noticed. Bending down, she put the tips of her fingers in its opening and traced them up the scratch and then down the other way.

Standing up, she turned and looked outside.

"Mom, what is this?" she asked.

Caroline turned her head. "I have no idea. I first found it yesterday. I don't know what it's from or how long it's been there."

"What's what?!" demanded Jackie, jumping from her seat to investigate.

Pushing her sister out of the doorway, Jackie knelt to examine the scratch.

Pulling back, she yelled, "Mom, did you tell the cop about this? This could be a clue."

Caroline had thought the same thing when she discovered it Saturday. It had to be new. She knew every part of that house and had never noticed it before. Deep down she knew it had to be related to the disappearance but didn't want to fully admit it to herself.

"Jackie, I don't know. Rose could have scratched the wall at some point and I just never noticed," Caroline replied. She didn't want to add fear to the situation. *Greg and Noel could walk in any minute, so why scare the girls more?* she thought.

"Let's call the police again and tell them. Maybe they can fingerprint it and run it through their like databases. I saw that on TV during the lockdown," Jackie replied.

"Jackie don't be dumb. That's not how it works," said Amanda.

"I'm not dumb. I was here. You took forever as always," snapped Jackie. "It's a possibility. At least I'm trying—not like you or Mom."

"Girls, just stop," Caroline chirped. She got up from her chair and walked to the scratch, rubbing her hand over it again.

"Mom, you are ruining all the DNA," Jackie whined. Amanda hit her arm and told her to shut up again.

Caroline rubbed the scratch one way and then the other. She leaned in close to examine its depth. It looked like a mighty fingernail scratch. Noel had just had her nails done. She thought back to that conversation when she first arrived.

"What on earth is wrong with your nails?" Caroline had asked.

"What? You don't like them?" Noel said and smirked. "You don't love long and orange? I thought the color was so fun and wanted to try something different."

Caroline liked a white or pink nail, and sometimes even a chic black, but the idea of orange made her wince.

"Get over it," Noel told her, pulling the bottle out of her pocket to show Caroline. "Lighten up, it's fun, and just nail polish. Not a tattoo."

"And we all know you have enough of those," Caroline retorted. "Ugh, and what's with all these rings these days?"

"I only have a few on," said Noel, slipping the bottle back into her jean pocket.

"Fine. But did you ever get the 'Loyola' tattoo removed?" Caroline asked. Noel had gotten it a few weeks after that night on the porch back in college to memorialize her first female love.

"I'll always love Loyola," she replied and winked.

Caroline remembered how it was just a few short days ago that they hugged and clasped hands to walk into the house to meet Rose and Greg. Noel's body was warm and soft. Over the years since college, her curvy frame stayed the same, yet it was more voluptuous with age.

It seemed so long ago now. Snapping back into the moment with the screech of Jackie's voice complaining yet again about DNA, she remembered that she had told Officer McKenna about the scratch.

"Maybe it's nothing to worry about and they'll be home tomorrow," Caroline followed up. "If they aren't, we'll talk with the police again."

CHAPTER 18

MOUNT KATAHDIN, MAINE

Sunday, May 9, at 4:46 p.m.

Marigold saw the man with the bike running up to where she and Marcus sat surrounded by blaring sirens. She knew by the way he was running that something wasn't right.

Marigold knew the man and had cleaned his room earlier that day. He came up to the inn every few months and was an incredibly neat guest, leaving almost nothing for her to do. Yet, he always left a fifty-dollar bill as a tip on the nightstand. He was always polite and would greet her in the hall with a smile and a kind word.

Looking at Marcus, she asked him what he thought was happening.

"I don't know," he replied. "This is wild."

As they watched Officer Kelly walk over to Chong, they knew something was horribly wrong in the way that he collapsed. Officer Kelly knelt beside him.

After a few moments, Officer Kelly waved another officer over to stay with Chong. He looked toward Marigold and Marcus and then began walking away from them up the street.

"Do you think it's the rest of the body?" Marigold asked Marcus.

"It could be. I don't know. This is some scary shit, girl," Marcus said and rested his hand on her shoulder, giving it a squeeze.

An officer ran to Chong. Marcus and Marigold watched the officer try to comfort him, but he was too distraught from what they could tell.

"Get me a cig," Marigold requested. Marcus obliged and pulled a pack from his back pocket, handing it to her.

"Do you think this is real? Or some sort of cruel joke?" he asked her as she began to smoke.

"This is real," she answered. "Do you have anything strong with you? I need a bump or a drink or something."

He shook his head and the two watched Officer Kelly as he became smaller and smaller.

* * * * *

Officer Kelly walked toward where the man said he had seen something terrible. He felt sick and his palms were sweating. *Please don't be another dead body*, he pleaded silently.

The wind kicked up the dust on the dirt road. It made Officer Kelly sneeze. He wanted to look back to see how far he had walked but didn't want his turning to be interpreted as weakness to the others waiting below. He kept walking.

Taking a few more strides, he pivoted from the center of the road closer to the grassy edge. And there it was. About fifteen feet in front of him, slightly peeking out around the width of a tree, a splash of red. Not a red that was natural to the forest but one distinctive of a golfer's polo-type shirt.

Officer Kelly took a few more steps forward and the scene began to come into focus. He didn't want to move too slowly so the crowd behind him would sense his fear. He was a cop. He was a good cop. And he was always meant to be a cop. This was his moment to be a true cop and solve a crime.

Stepping into the grass, he crept cautiously toward the tree. What if there was a bear around? They were sometimes seen, especially close to the mountain like this. *Worse yet*, he thought, *what if the person who had done this was still here? Still here and watching.* He froze for a brief second thinking about it.

You have to keep going, he told himself and took a deep breath, crossing himself again with his right hand. The red was larger now, and he could make out the shape of a man. He was handsome, middle-aged, tall, and thin. Moving closer, he bent down to examine the man a bit more. He wore a red polo shirt and dark blue jeans.

He didn't look so bad. Officer Kelly thought that all dead bodies were going to be black and bloated based on pictures he saw in the academy. But this man looked almost like he was awake but calm with this open eyes gazing off into the distance. Bending over him a bit closer, Officer Kelly scrutinized his face, up one side, down the other. He looked at his shoulders, his chest. He scanned down his arms.

He was married based on the thin gold band on his left hand. He was thin but well sculpted. He seemed like the type of guy you'd meet for beers and have a few laughs with, but he wouldn't get too drunk or laugh too hard and would still be home in bed by a reasonable hour. Maybe a woman would try to pick him up, but he'd politely decline.

Officer Kelly stopped for a second realizing how silly it was to speculate about the man. He was dead. He'd never have beers with him. This man would never have a beer again with anyone. But who was he and how did he get here behind a tree, dead in nowhere Maine?

Officer Kelly stood up and tried to shake his childish thoughts about the handsome dead man. Then it occurred to him. Her other half must be nearby. Not another full person. Just a half to match the rest of the body down the road.

Turning slowly, he saw it between two pine trees. The legs were at least six feet away. Walking closer to them, he noticed that they had no shoes, just bare feet.

Scanning the feet, he noticed the orange toenails, the same color that matched the other half down the road on the woman's hands. Noticing her legs attached to her hips, he made the realization that she had been cut in half. Cut in half like what they do in fake magic tricks.

But this wasn't fake like magic. This was real. Half of her was here and the other half someplace else. Who would have done this? Who would have cut this woman in half? And why? Feeling overwhelmed and sick again, Officer Kelly took a few steps back. He realized he may be damaging any evidence. There was nothing else there that he could tell. Just a dead man and half a woman.

"Man, what the fuck? Are you okay? What's over here?" yelled another officer as he walked up the road toward Officer Kelly with an ambulance driver. "This is some sick shit."

Officer Kelly nodded and headed back toward the street. "I wouldn't go up there if I were you. I think we need to call in some more help or something. Did anyone call the medical inspector? Should we call down to Portland to get someone up here to investigate further? They must have just been dropped. It doesn't look like any animals have touched them."

The officer nodded, and he and the ambulance driver peered around Officer Kelly.

"Like I said, I wouldn't go up there just yet, man," he said and began walking back down the street, unsure of what to do next.

CHAPTER 19

NEWBURYPORT, MASSACHUSETTS

Caroline, Noel, and Greg,
two years ago from today

Caroline was in the kitchen fixing dinner for her and Greg. He had been traveling and working like crazy, and she missed having him home. She spent the afternoon making popovers, his favorite, and a potato casserole.

She bought some lobsters and had a steak on the grill. For the surf-and-turf feast, she bought a bottle of vodka. Greg loved a dirty martini after traveling. He wasn't a big drinker but could appreciate a well-made martini every so often.

Caroline set the table and poured herself a glass of wine. It was almost 6:00 p.m. He had texted her a few hours prior, letting her know he'd be home around then. Caroline had a small bubble of excitement building in her stomach about his return. She missed him and was excited to hear about his trip.

At 6:00 p.m., there was no Greg. She texted him, "Will you be home soon?" Ten minutes went by. No answer. Caroline poured herself another glass of wine and put the plates in the oven to keep the dinner warm.

At 6:17 p.m., she called him. It went directly to voicemail. Caroline went to the front window in the living room to watch for his car. Rose paced behind her. Moving from the window to the couch, she propped herself up on a few pillows so she could keep one eye on the driveway.

At 7:00 p.m., she called him again. Still voicemail. She debated having her own meal alone but decided to wait. Maybe there was traffic. Maybe his BMW was having a problem again and wouldn't start at the airport.

Caroline decided she'd start on her lobster and seated herself at the table, picking over the lukewarm food with Rose now at her feet. The time ticked by. Still no Greg.

Reaching for her phone, she called Noel. There was no answer. She called Jackie, no answer. She called Amanda, no answer. A feeling of loneliness crept in. She had missed Greg and was excited for him to get home. That upcoming weekend, they had planned on going to the golf course on Saturday and meeting another couple for brunch on Sunday.

The ringing phone interrupted Caroline's thoughts about the weekend ahead. It was Noel.

"Hi there," she chirped, excited to hear Noel's voice.

"Hey girl, how are you?" Noel responded. "What's cracking in your world?"

Caroline could barely hear her. There were people talking and a hum in the background. She told Noel about the problem with Greg bailing on her for the weekend.

"Oh, I'm at the airport. Last-minute trip to Georgia for the weekend," she said.

"What's in Georgia?" asked Caroline, surprised to hear about her friend's last-minute trip. "Greg's on his way home from there. He had a sales meeting. I thought he'd be home by now but looks like something's come up. I haven't heard from him, and he's still not home," said Caroline.

"Oh weird," answered Noel.

Caroline, still curious, pushed her friend. "Who are you going with to Georgia? What's down there?"

"No one you know," replied Noel. "I need to go, though. Trying to get through security. Have a great weekend, baby. See ya."

Caroline was surprised at the prompt exit from the conversation. Placing the phone down, she reached for the wine. It was almost 8:00 p.m. and still no Greg.

Just then, the phone rang. Greg's name graced her phone screen. She hit the button to answer.

"Greg, where are you?" she asked.

"Hey, babe, I'm not going to make it home. I have to stay in Georgia. The customer wants to go golfing here this weekend, and I'm right on the run for a hot deal. I can't leave. I'm sorry. I know we had plans this weekend."

Caroline's heart broke. Rose sensed it and moved closer to her.

"Okay, that's fine," she replied. It wasn't. She was so hurt.

"Are you mad?" he asked.

"No," she said. "No, I'm not."

"I'll make it up to you. I promise," he said.

"Okay, sure," she said. He began to say something else, but she hung up before she could hear what he had to say.

She put the phone down and picked up the wine glass, finishing it off. He had done this once, maybe twice before. *How could he just abandon her like this?*

She started to really get angry. And then she got even angrier that her friend had rushed her off the phone, too. The wine was running through her veins and the bubble of excitement burst, releasing rage through her body. It tingled. She couldn't stand it.

Picking up the wine glass, she flung it across the room, hitting a picture of the family framing the wall next to the television. Concerned about Rose stepping on the glass, she guided the dog up the stairs with her, shutting the bedroom door behind them.

The next morning, she awoke with a headache and slumped down the stairs. Seeing the glass spread across the room, she questioned how much wine she'd actually had. Picking up the pieces gingerly, she began to wonder why she was so angry.

Caroline was angry at Greg's last-minute change and decision to stay in Georgia. She understood that clients' needs were something he cared deeply about, along with ensuring that his relationships stayed strong. But this was something new with the last-minute changes.

When she married Greg, she thought over time she'd fall more in love with him. When she found out she was pregnant and he was so excited, she thought that'd help, too. While she loved Greg, it wasn't the type of love she had imagined as a young girl.

And maybe it didn't need to be. Maybe it was okay that she cared for him and loved him, but it wasn't that wild, crazy, sexy, romantic love you see in movies, not the way she had loved Matt. But she was young then, and this was now.

Caroline walked to the kitchen, the glass shards chipping at her hands. Dumping the glass in the trash, she went back to pick up more. She thought again about her anger. Maybe it was due to the girls moving on with their lives and moving out.

Once they finished college, they both came back and lived with her and Greg for a few years, but now they were out on their own, and that put the focus on her and Greg spending more time together and talking more.

It felt empty. Caroline began writing more for the local paper and was starting to write for national publications, too. She was on social media more reuniting with friends and even looked Matt up a few times.

He was living in California and was divorced with two sons around her daughters' ages at twenty-seven. She'd delete her search history after she snooped in case Greg logged in to one of her accounts by mistake. She could never get into his, though. It didn't matter. They knew all the same people on there anyway.

CHAPTER 20

MOUNT KATAHDIN, MAINE

Sunday, May 9, at 5:02 p.m.

Dr. Isaac was a medical inspector who was heading up from Portland on Sunday evening after he received a call that two bodies had been found near Mount Katahdin in grotesque condition. After packing up the car with a few essentials for the drive and the overnight, he kissed his wife, Pam, goodbye, and she wished him luck.

Standing in the garage of their waterfront condo, he wondered what was ahead of him. He had spoken to one gentleman from the hospital and an Officer Kelly, who would meet him there. Officer Kelly sounded upset on the phone and didn't get into too much detail.

Dr. Isaac was familiar with tough examinations. He had lived in DC, LA, and Boston throughout his career, and had grown used to seeing tattered and torn bodies from accidents, murders, and illnesses. He had written books on his experiences and even had appeared on several true crime television shows over the years.

But now in his early sixties, he was tired of seeing the worst done to people by the worst people. He was volunteering his time at the local hospital and homeless shelters and was taking up sailing with Pam. She told him it was good for him. He had also begun walking with her to lose some extra weight.

He had promised her a year ago when he retired that he'd lose the weight and spend more time with her. And he was delivering on it. She had always been so patient with his career and with raising their children while he carved out a reputation for himself in the medical world.

Looking at his GPS, he was hoping to arrive at the Mount Katahdin hospital by 9:30 p.m. The car ride was relaxing, although he wished that Pam had come for the trip. He was going to stay at an inn where Officer Kelly had secured him a room.

Arriving at the hospital earlier than what he expected, he noticed a cruiser parked at the front entrance. A young man paced back and forth in front of it. Parking his Jaguar in an open space, he got out of the car with his medical bag and walked toward the young man.

"Good evening," Dr. Isaac began and reached his hand out. "Are you Officer Kelly?"

Officer Kelly nodded. "Yes, I am. You must be Dr. Isaac."

"Why yes, I am," he said and chuckled, then pushed his glasses back up the bridge of his nose. "What can I do for you?"

The two began to walk into the hospital as Officer Kelly explained the situation in more detail. Dr. Isaac nodded in agreement as he spoke. He knew that two dead bodies had been found and brought to the hospital, but not much more.

As they arrived at the hospital morgue door, Officer Kelly stopped and wiped his head. "What's the matter, son?" inquired Dr. Isaac, pushing his own long white hair back.

"Well, uh, you see," he began. "One's in half."

"In half?" Dr. Isaac asked, surprised at the statement. He had seen many terrible situations, but only once did he ever see a body cut in two.

"Yes, it's in half," Officer Kelly said again, opening the door to let Dr. Isaac head in first. The doctor in the room introduced himself, but swiftly left when Dr. Isaac entered, leaving him and Officer Kelly with the two people covered by sheets.

Dr. Isaac placed his bag down and headed to the sink to wash his hands and prepare.

"Son, you don't need to stay. I can do the examination and write up my report and get everything in line for you," Dr. Isaac said.

"No, I think I want to stay," Officer Kelly answered sheepishly. "I feel like I kind of owe it to them to be here the entire time."

Dr. Isaac nodded. "Who's under which sheet?"

Officer Kelly told him that the man was on the right, the woman on the left. Dr. Isaac nodded. "Let's start with him first."

Carefully pulling the sheet back, he noticed, too, how handsome the man was, with salt-and-pepper hair that needed a trim and a light tan to his skin. Pulling the sheet further down, he admired the man's well-toned chest for a man his age. Scanning him up and down, he couldn't quite yet tell what had killed him.

Officer Kelly paced on the opposite side of the room.

"You okay, son?" asked Dr. Isaac. Officer Kelly nodded.

Dr. Isaac began examining the body closely as Officer Kelly continued to watch. "Any major marks or identifiers?" Dr. Isaac asked.

"He has a yellow cartoon-like bird tattoo on his butt cheek," Officer Kelly answered.

Dr. Isaac chuckled. He moved to the man's head, moving the tufts of hair from side to side. And there it was. A hole. He leaned in closer.

"Son, did anyone mention this?" he asked, still inspecting.

"Mention what?" inquired Officer Kelly.

"Come look," he replied, waving Officer Kelly over. Officer Kelly stood next to Dr. Isaac and leaned in. He gasped when he saw it.

"It looks like a small bullet hole, like a twenty-two millimeter," Officer Kelly stated as he moved his face closer. Then, realizing what he was looking at, jumped back. Dr. Isaac laughed.

"He won't bite, son" said Dr. Isaac. "I know you mentioned that the toxicology and the lab test results will be in tomorrow. But any idea who this man is?"

Officer Kelly shook his head. "No, no one around here knows him. We thought maybe a tourist or someone just passing through. But he's no local. Neither is the lady."

"Speaking of her, let's check her out," Dr. Isaac replied, somewhat dreading to see a severed body yet somewhat excited to see it, especially at this point in his career. He covered the man with the sheet and moved over to where the woman was on the opposite table.

The two halves of her were under the sheet on a single table, as if she were still a whole woman placed in the correct order. Pulling the sheet back, Dr. Isaac was met with the face of a somewhat attractive, yet quirky-looking woman.

Her red hair was curly and her face appeared to be kind. While always trying to be professional, Dr. Isaac liked to imagine the people he examined in happier times. He imagined her on a beach in Greece laughing with friends.

Moving from her face, her neck showed a story far different from the cries of laughter on a *Mediterranean* beach. Violent marks of purple and red lined her throat like a choker necklace. It was so violent it looked to be fake, like poorly done Halloween makeup of someone trying to mimic the same look.

He stood back, pausing to consider this beautiful woman's face held up by a violently torn neck. He then moved to her hands. Her fingernails were painted and the polish was chipped. Her nails were broken and scratches marked the skin. Dr. Isaac looked carefully at each one, noticing specs of white paint under a few of the nails.

"Same thing about her? No one knows her?" Dr. Isaac asked Officer Kelly.

"Same thing," Officer Kelly said. "Oh yeah, before you ask, she's got a few tattoos on her back, too."

"Of what?" asked Dr. Isaac.

"One tattoo is of a name—a name I don't know how to say. The others are just designs. A flower, a map of Italy, and a strange, flower-like design, and maybe like a butterfly," Officer Kelly answered.

She looked like she would have tattoos, Dr. Isaac thought to himself, *unlike the man with the cartoon bird tattoo.* Looking back down at her, he looked at her breasts that, even with her age, still had a lovely shape to them. He assumed she had never had children as there wasn't any sagging or stretch marks.

"Son, you may want to look away," he said. "I'll be pulling the sheet down further and you may not want to see this."

"I want to stay," Officer Kelly said.

"Fair enough," Dr. Isaac replied.

Pulling the sheet down to her feet, he paused when he first saw the separation of the parts of her body. He thought about her figure and how she would have looked dancing on those Greek islands. Examining the severed section, it looked raw and violent. More violent than the choking marks around her neck. He then remembered Officer Kelly.

"You still good?" Dr. Isaac asked, not even bothering to look up.

He heard a faint, "Yeah," and kept looking at her severed sections. Glancing down at the second part, her legs and feet all looked somewhat normal considering the situation. He moved back up to her curly locks and began running his gloved fingers through her hair, looking for a similar hole but felt nothing.

His eyes, although professionally trained and accustomed to seeing bodies like this, kept darting back to where she had been separated. Moving back to examine it, he ran his fingers across both sides of both sections. The cut that was done on her was rough, like someone using pinking shears along construction paper.

"Do a lot of woodcutters live around here?" he asked.

He knew the answer was yes. On the drive up, he made a game of counting how many logging trucks he passed. It was at least seven. Plus, he had read an article in one of the Maine lifestyle magazines that focused on a "day in the life" and the most recent one was of a man who cut down trees full-time and explained his love of chainsaws.

"Yes, sir," replied Officer Kelly, now facing the wall, unable to look at the body the way that Dr. Isaac could.

"Are there any really bad ones up here?" asked Dr. Isaac. "Like guys who are lumberjacks, who you can just tell are bad dudes?"

"Yes, sir," replied Officer Kelly again. He could feel his phone vibrating in his pocket and knew it was Emma. He wanted to talk to her so bad but couldn't just yet. It was the sixth call he had ignored.

"Some of the guys are really bad, like former felons who come up here to get work since they can't do anything else. We know that some of them transport drugs under the logs between here and Canada, and even further north in Maine. A few of them cause some other troubles around town and commit petty theft. But what does that have to do with this? You think a logger did it?" Officer Kelly asked.

Dr. Isaac shook his head. "Not sure, but maybe. You may want to get a list together of all the 'bad' ones and start finding out more about their routes lately, if no one knows these two people. That may help you," offered Dr. Isaac.

Dr. Isaac knew that wasn't part of his job but could tell that Officer Kelly was new to this and nervous. He wanted to help.

"I'd say someone cut her across the middle at her waist here with a chainsaw," he said and motioned his arm across as Officer Kelly turned to view the gesture. "I want to look at her more throughout the night to understand what her body, and his, are telling me."

"So, should I wait to hear from you in the morning once you get the lab work?" asked Officer Kelly.

He nodded yes, and as Officer Kelly headed out of the room, Dr. Isaac said, "Oh, and son, I won't be needing that room tonight."

CHAPTER 21

BEACON HILL, BOSTON, MASSACHUSETTS

Caroline and Greg, twenty-eight years ago

The week before Greg and Caroline were married, he had left for the weekend for his bachelor party. The two had been living in Boston. Greg was an analyst for a financial firm and was considering getting into the medical device industry. Caroline was working as an assistant at a publishing company and freelance writing on the side.

Greg's aunt had a house in Charlestown and turned part of the home into an apartment, which the two jumped at the chance to live in after graduating from college.

During their first official night in the city, they decided to take a swan boat ride. It was a chilly May night and they were the only two on the boat besides the driver. During the ride, Caroline snuggled into Greg's arms and thought about their love. She loved him. He was dependable as they transitioned from college life to being "real" adults. She just thought it would be different, that it would feel different.

Now, over a year later, Greg was kissing her again on his way to his bachelor party with friends for the Memorial Day weekend. They were headed to Nantucket to boat and drink. Caroline figured Nantucket was the most respectable place for them to go—no strip clubs among the proper and rich.

As Greg put a few more things in his bag and mulled around the apartment pre-gaming with a beer, Caroline looked up from her book.

"Greg," she began.

"Yeah, babe?" he said, pausing mid-step.

"Are you happy to be getting married?" she asked, needing some reassurance prior to his departure. She had a weekend full of reading and last-minute wedding errands to run. Plus, they were going to Bermuda for their honeymoon so she still had some packing to do.

"I can't wait," he replied and resumed his step.

"Greg," she said again.

"Yeah, babe," he said, pausing again.

"Are you excited to be marrying me?" she asked. She knew he'd say yes. But she needed to hear it from him so she could replay this moment in her head over and over throughout the weekend for the constant reassurance.

Greg looked surprised. He put the beer on the counter and walked over to Caroline's perch on the couch. Sitting next to her, he pulled her legs across his body and moved her onto his lap.

"What's going on? Why are you asking this?" he said, looking concerned. "Of course I'm excited to be marrying you."

Caroline put her book to the side, then placed her head on Greg's shoulder. "I guess it's just pre-wedding jitters," she explained.

He nodded. "You know, I've never told you this. But I've loved you since the day I saw you, in that dank bar back at school. I knew the moment I looked at you that you were the one."

Caroline pulled back. This was too much. He had never told her that ever. "You did?" she finally said.

"I did," he said, pulling her head close to his. "And that night at the pizza place, the way you looked under those soft lights correcting me on our pizza choice, that was it. I knew that for the rest of my life, I wanted you telling me I was wrong and correcting my choice of pizza."

Caroline laughed while a tear bubbled in one eye. "You jerk," she said, playfully hitting his chest.

"Are you nervous about me going away for the weekend? Caroline, nothing's going to happen, it's just a stupid boys' weekend. We're gonna have some beers, go out on Johnny's boat, and play golf. Nothing to worry about," he said.

"I know," Caroline replied. The sentiments that he had shared were more than reassurance to her about his feelings, but a nagging in her stomach was still there.

He kissed her head and wiggled out from under her.

"I need to get ready. Johnny and Noel will be here soon."

Caroline was shocked.

"Wait, Noel?" she asked.

"Yeah, she's in town and wants to go down with us for the night. Come on, Caroline, you know Noel. She's like one of the boys and I've known her forever. I didn't think it was a big deal," replied Greg.

"Are you kidding me?" Caroline asked, still shocked at the news.

"No, not a big deal," said Greg. As he replied, they heard a horn beep.

Greg walked to the window and looked out.

"They're here," said Greg. "I gotta go."

Caroline walked Greg to the door, waving at Johnny and Noel from the doorway and trying to hide her shock. Greg kissed her one last time.

"Bye, babe, I love you," he said, and ran down the steps, disappearing into Johnny's Bronco.

The following Tuesday, Greg moved up the stairs with a lot less enthusiasm. Caroline met him at the door. They hadn't talked all weekend. But Noel had called a few times and left messages on the answering machine that they were having fun and there was nothing to worry about.

"Tired?" she asked.

He nodded. Walking into the apartment, he dropped his bag in the kitchen.

"Babe, I have something to tell you," he began. Caroline, who had spent the weekend drinking white wine spritzers with friends and running a few less errands than she had hoped for, froze. Did he cheat on her? What did he have to say?

"What is it?" she asked.

Greg turned his back, unbuckled his belt, and pulled his jeans and boxers down. There, staring at Caroline, was something so surprising she almost spit up the sip of wine she took. On Greg's butt cheek was a small yellow cartoon bird tattoo.

"A cartoon bird?" she exclaimed. "You got a yellow cartoon bird? And on your butt?"

"Yes, I got a tattoo," he said and laughed as he pulled up his pants.

"They have tattoo places on Nantucket?" she asked, confused about how it got there.

"Uh no, but I lost a bet on the way down, so we stopped in Providence for me to get this," he explained.

"What was the bet?" she asked.

"The bet was, I thought I could go the entire weekend without talking about you," he began. "The guys said up to three times all weekend was the cutoff point. I got to three times before we left Essex county, so the first place we saw, we stopped, and I got this."

Caroline was both confused and flattered. "So now we have to look at this for the rest of our lives together?" she asked.

"I'm afraid so," he replied.

CHAPTER 22

MOUNT KATAHDIN, MAINE

Sunday, May 9, at 7:14 p.m.

"Pour me five fingers," Marigold instructed Marcus. He did, and then poured some whiskey into his own glass. A neighbor brought the twins to the inn because Marigold didn't want to go home. She didn't want to be at the inn either, having to stare across the road at where she had found a body hours earlier. But she didn't want to be alone.

The twins were asleep in a guest room. Marcus agreed to stay with her. He, too, was shaken by everything that had happened. Chong, the New York lawyer who had found the other body, had tried to leave the inn to head back to Albany.

When Officer Kelly walked him, Marcus, and Marigold back to the safety of the inn's walls, Chong begged Officer Kelly to let him drive home. Officer Kelly told him no, he needed to stay while they collected evidence to understand who these people were and what happened to them. Chong wouldn't be going anywhere anytime soon.

Unlike Chong, Marcus and Marigold were used to the confines of the inn. But they were not used to this feeling of dread, so unlike the normal day-to-day feeling that accompanied them everywhere. This type of dread was deeper, darker than the dread that comes with making the same beds each and every day and engaging in small talk with tourists over Maine blueberry muffins.

The two asked Chong if he wanted to sit with them and have a drink. Distraught, he declined and stumbled up the stairs to the darkness of the second floor and the comfort of his own room. Both were curious as to what he had seen compared to them.

Talking a deep drink of the whiskey, Marigold shook her head. "How the fuck do you think they got here? What type of monster would do that to people?"

Marcus shrugged. "No fucking clue. And why here? Out of all the places in the blessed world, why here? In the middle of nowhere?"

"That's exactly why. It's the middle of nowhere," Marigold answered. The two took sips of their respective drinks.

"May I join you?" asked a voice. Looking behind them, there stood Chong. He had showered and changed clothes. His face was bloated and red. Marigold nodded and pulled out the chair next to her, gesturing for him to sit down. He did.

"Do you want a drink?" asked Marcus, holding the bottle up and waving it from side to side.

Chong nodded. "Just a little," he said.

Marcus pulled a glass from the cabinet and poured Chong the remaining whiskey.

Reaching for the glass, Chong took a sip and shuddered. Marigold reached out, hitting Chong's back. "Drink up. You deserve it."

The three sat there quietly staring into their glasses, no one willing to break the awkward silence. Marcus started first.

"You're the lawyer, right? You come up every few months and ride your bike?" he asked.

Chong nodded. "Yes, I've been coming up for years. I've seen you both here forever. It's nice to finally talk to you."

Marcus and Marigold nodded. He had never tried before to speak to Marigold, and she was fairly sure he'd never spoken to Marcus either, outside of pleasantries to both.

More silence. More sips of hot and heavy whiskey. More niceties about the area and its extreme beauty. Finally, Marigold got annoyed. She wanted to know. She wanted to know so bad if his experience was worse than hers.

"What did you see?" she finally asked. Marcus shushed her.

"Shut up," she told him.

Chong sighed.

"I knew that was coming," he said.

He pushed the pads of his fingers across his forehead as if summoning the memory that he was trying too hard to forget already.

"It was the strangest thing," he began. "I was riding my bike and knew I didn't have much further to go, but thought I'd stop just for a moment and sit to reflect on my day and hydrate."

Marcus and Marigold put their drinks down, both listening intently for what he was going to say next. Chong took a final sip, placing the now-empty glass on the counter.

"Then, I was sitting there and noticed something behind a tree. I thought maybe it was a bird or piece of trash," he explained. "I decided to check it out. I thought if it was trash, I'd pick it up and throw it away when I got the bottom of the mountain."

Marigold was getting impatient. Who cared about the trash? She raised her glass and spun it in circles to encourage Chong to go on. He took the hint.

"And there it was," he said. "A man."

"A man?" cried Marcus and Marigold at the same time.

"Yes," answered Chong. "He was middle-aged-ish and quite handsome. He had a red shirt on. I can't tell what killed him. In some ways, he looked so peaceful, yet he was dead and I knew it wasn't good."

Marcus and Marigold knew that he saw something terrible, and Officer Kelly had been coy in telling them what Chong saw as he rushed them away from the scene of the crime.

"Then I turned and thought I saw two white boards," he continued. "And it turned out to be," he paused to catch his breath, "the bottom half of a woman."

Silence followed.

After a few moments, Marigold opened her mouth. "Well, I found the other half of her," she said.

Chong turned to her looking awestruck yet again.

"Not good," replied Marigold.

"No, not good at all," agreed Chong.

CHAPTER 23

NEWBURYPORT, MASSACHUSETTS

Sunday, May 9,
at 8:08 p.m.

On Sunday evening, Jackie found herself wrapped in a thick comforter in her childhood room. As she scrolled through one of her social media accounts, her new boyfriend, Rick, who she had met on a dating site, texted her to see if she'd be around Monday night for dinner. She ignored it. How would she ever explain to anyone, let alone a new guy, that her father just disappeared with her mother's friend?

She continued to scroll. She wasn't sure if Rick was the one. Jackie had excused herself to her room to think about the day and how unimaginable it all seemed. How do two people just disappear like that?

Her mother was acting cold and aloof, more so than usual. And now that Amanda arrived, she could take a moment away and let her handle their mother. She heard a knock at the door a few moments later.

"Come in," she said, hoping it wasn't her mother. The door opened and Amanda slipped through and walked over to her tightly wrapped sister.

Amanda began. "What in the hell is going on here?"

Jackie put down her phone. "I have no friggin' clue," she answered.

Amanda held the stare.

"I mean, let's be honest, and I can't say this to Mom, but do you think Dad ran off with Noel?" asked Amanda. Her mind was fixated on that moment as a child when she saw the two together. She'd felt unsettled about it ever since.

"Don't be dumb," snapped Jackie. "Never in a million years would Dad leave Mom for Noel. She's a fucking space clown and so out of her head all the time with that whack hair and weird clothes and nails. Dad's way too refined to leave Mom for someone like Noel."

"You are so rude," replied Amanda. "Noel is so kind and warm—not like Mom. And you don't know. None of us know. It could happen."

Amanda so badly wanted to tell her sister about the encounter from her childhood and find out if Jackie had ever seen or sensed anything similar between their father and Noel, or even another woman. But Jackie's response led her to think otherwise.

Jackie, now feeling triggered by Amanda's comments, wanted to dig.

"Why would you even say that? Do you think Dad cheats on Mom?" asked Jackie.

"Do you?" Amanda retorted.

Jackie looked at her, shocked. She had never considered it. But based on her sister's response, something felt off. "No," she replied coldly.

"You are just like Mom," Amanda said.

"I am not. Unlike Mom, I'd be pushing the police to get out there and search for them. I don't have an ounce of pushover the way that she does," Jackie explained.

Amanda wished she and her sister got along better. Or at least saw eye to eye every so often. So badly she wanted to tell her about the encounter so many years ago. Did that matter? Would that matter?

Looking out the window, she noticed the lights go out in the neighbor's bedroom next door. She debated about telling her sister.

"Do you have anything else to say? Or are you just here to annoy me?" Jackie asked.

Amanda shook her head. She had left their mother propped on a chair in the screened-in porch. When her wine had run out, she had begun to open up to Amanda.

"Mom said that Dad's been acting kind of weird. And he's extended a few business trips to last all weekend," said Amanda.

"So? Dad really cares about his work," replied Jackie.

Amanda shook her head. "Mom thought it was more than that. She was thinking about posting something on her social media account about them being missing and that maybe someone's seen them or something," Amanda said.

"That's nuts. Why would Mom air that dirty laundry out to the world?" asked Jackie.

"They could be home tomorrow and this is some awful misunderstanding. The whole world doesn't need to know that. People will think we're nuts."

"Maybe," replied Amanda. "But maybe it will help."

Frustrated with her sister, who was back to scrolling on her phone, Amanda headed to her own room down the hall. As she walked, the smiling faces of her and her family on the walls guided her to the comfort of her childhood bed.

Lying in bed, staring out the window, she couldn't stop herself from thinking about her father and if he was truly the way she thought he was.

CHAPTER 24

MOUNT KATAHDIN, MAINE

Monday, May 10,
at 6:00 a.m.

D r. Isaac had spent the night closely examining the bodies. Up the one, down the other. Down the one, up the other. He examined their hands, their teeth, their toes. He massaged their cold heads feeling for bumps and holes. He felt as if he knew them intimately by the time dawn broke.

At 6:00 a.m., he began to write a detailed overview of each corpse, detailing the moles, the tattoos, and his conclusion on what the causes of death were for both.

A nurse brought the lab results in around 7:00 a.m. Reading them over, Dr. Isaac added to his report to further understand what happened and confirm whether there were any toxins or abnormalities in the blood. For the most part, it was clean minus some slight alcohol readings.

At 8:30 a.m., he was still finishing some notes. His wife had called a few times, but he ignored the calls, trying not to break his concentration. But a few minutes later, Officer Kelly called. He knew he needed to give him an update.

"Hello," he answered.

"Hi there," greeted Officer Kelly. "What's it looking like?"

"Why don't you come on down?" said Dr. Isaac. "Probably better for us to talk about in person."

* * * * *

A half hour later, Officer Kelly walked into a makeshift office that the hospital staff had set up for Dr. Isaac. Officer Kelly was thankful he didn't have to see the corpses again. Motioning Officer Kelly to take a seat, Dr. Isaac passed him a copy of the report.

He began to flip through it, unsure of what he was reading. He hadn't slept all night and his excitement of telling Emma about all the happenings had backfired. She was scared. She was scared for him and his safety, and she was scared to visit during the upcoming weekend if they thought there was a killer on the loose. Officer Kelly was not only exhausted but sad about what this situation could potentially mean for his relationship.

"Don't bother reading through the whole thing," advised Dr. Isaac. "A lot of it won't make sense to you."

Officer Kelly knew Dr. Isaac didn't say it to be a jerk but because it would be easier to talk through the report rather than pretend he knew what he was looking at.

Officer Kelly quickly dropped the report, abiding by Dr. Isaac's comment.

"Listen, son. I've seen a lot of dead bodies and have written thousands of these reports. But this is somewhat unique," explained Dr. Isaac. Officer Kelly tensed up, nervous about what Dr. Isaac was going to say next.

"Let me give you the list since I know you are new to this," said Dr. Isaac. "It looks like both were relatively healthy people. There are no major toxicology issues in the blood, minus a smidge of alcohol. But nothing major. For the man, it looks like he was shot in the head with a small bullet from a small gun. Like a pistol. We'll have to look at that more."

Dr. Isaac paused, taking a sip of water. Officer Kelly's heart began to beat harder, knowing that they'd be talking next about the woman.

"For him," he began, "I think it was quick. And the sole bullet did the job. I'd say for him he was killed around 11:00 p.m. the night before, judging from the body. For her, it was a bit more gruesome, as we know. I'm assuming the person, or persons, who did this strangled her first. But my assumption is that once she was dead from strangulation, they needed a way to dispose of the body. So, cutting her in half was a way to do that in an attempt to destroy further evidence of identifying who she was."

Dr. Isaac paused, as if waiting to see if Officer Kelly had any questions. He didn't so he just nodded as he visualized the situation and the fear that these people must have felt.

Taking the hint, Dr. Isaac continued.

"I'd say she was killed after him. They did a sloppy job at cutting her in half," he said then paused to take a drink to clear his throat and to push his glasses and white hair back.

"In reviewing her sides, it looks like they started with a knife, but it became too much work. It would be hard for anyone to slice someone in half, let alone with a knife only," Dr. Isaac said.

Officer Kelly cringed but tried his hardest to hide it.

"But as they cut, they moved to another options, something stronger," Dr. Isaac explained. "I'm assuming it was a chainsaw due to the nature of the larger part of the cut and the intensity of the marks along her body separating one half from the other."

Dr. Isaac paused again. Officer Kelly wondered if he noticed the way he had twinged. He felt sick to his stomach.

"Do you need a drink of water?" Dr. Isaac asked.

Officer Kelly shook his head.

"I'd say whoever did this was a bit of a novice and didn't have a clear plan based on the variants in methods between guns to knives to something fiercer. As I said, I'd say they wanted to dispose of the body, hence the cut, but maybe became too afraid, which is why they dumped one half here and then the other so close down the street from the other half," he paused. "I am surprised that they were so sloppy, but again shows that this is not something professional but something more spur of the moment."

Officer Kelly nodded, not sure of what to do next. Dr. Isaac continued.

"Son, you have no idea about who these people could be?" he asked.

Officer Kelly shook his head again.

"I can connect you with some other experts to speak with, but I do think you should start sharing with all the media outlets renditions of their faces and identifiers on their bodies to see if anyone can identify them. Maybe that will help and you'll find out who these people are. At least that way, you'll be able to further figure out what happened to them and how they got all the way up here," said Dr. Isaac.

Officer Kelly nodded. Getting up, he reached his hand out to shake Dr. Isaac's hand, thanking him with a weak voice.

Dr. Isaac told Officer Kelly that he was happy to help, and Officer Kelly felt like he truly meant it. He felt in no way prepared to take on such a huge case and wished Dr. Isaac could stay. But he could see the doctor was glad to be done with this horrific case and happy to be heading back to his home in Portland.

CHAPTER 25

NEWBURYPORT, MASSACHUSETTS

Monday, May 10, at 7:08 a.m.

Caroline woke up Monday morning to a feeling of absolute dread in her stomach. That, paired with the pounding in her head from the wine, left her unable to move or think.

Shuffling to the bathroom a few minutes later, she glanced out the window on her way. The girls' cars were still in the driveway, but no other sign of life or of Greg and Noel outside. Turning the shower on, she let it warm while she ventured down the stairs to check if they were there and to also let Rose out.

There was Rose, anxious to run out into the yard, but nothing else differed compared to the night before. Leaving the door open for Rose to come back in when she was done with her business, Caroline went back up the stairs and into the steaming bathroom and shower.

She began to strategize as she washed her hair. The police were of no help. The girls were scared although not showing it. She thought back to the suggestion of posting something on social media about this strange occurrence but shook away the thought. *What if the two ran off together?* The thought trailed across her mind. *How embarrassing that would be to openly look for help via social media just to be met with the sad outcome of being a scorned and lonely woman?*

But maybe that wasn't such a bad idea. Greg used social media a lot and was always on her account and on his. He loved the golf memes and posting pictures of the girls when they were younger. He had several hundred friends, both work and personal ones, unlike Caroline who only had one hundred or so.

As she rinsed her hair, she thought about what she'd write. Something like, "Hi friends, has anyone seen Noel and Greg?" *No,* she thought. *That would sound awful.* Maybe something more along the lines of, "I'm quite concerned as my friend and husband went missing on Saturday night. If you see them, please reach out," and she'd attach a recent picture from when Noel arrived on Saturday, as the three had taken a selfie.

You could clearly see Noel's and Greg's faces while Caroline's was cut off along the side. It would give people an idea about who they were and what they were wearing.

Ugh, but that terrible nail polish, thought Caroline. *But it was such an obnoxious color, maybe that would help, too.*

She wrapped herself in a luxe towel as she got out of the shower and put the toilet seat down. Caroline knew that putting something on social media could help her get control of the situation. Rubbing her head, she decided to tell the girls.

She put her robe on and walked down the hall, stopping midway between the two rooms.

"Girls," Caroline started.

"Yes, Mom?" Jackie said from her bed, as Amanda came out of her room.

"I think I'm going to post something on social media, just to see if that helps," she said.

"Good idea," reassured Amanda as she wrapped her arms around her mother.

"I'm calling out of work," replied Jackie. "But yeah, Mom, time to take control. Post it on Dad's social media page, too. Do you have Noel's login to do hers, too?"

That thought had never crossed Caroline's mind, but it made sense. She could always tag herself on both posts so people could message her directly. She and the girls went downstairs to the living room to collect the family laptop. Caroline sat in the middle with one girl on each side. She logged in to the computer and opened up the browser to her social media page.

"How do I do this?" Caroline asked.

Amanda pulled the laptop onto her own lap and began to write a post. "How about this?" she said as she typed.

Reading it over, Caroline thought it was okay. Jackie peered over her mother's shoulder and told her it read terribly. She pulled the laptop from her mother and sister and began typing feverishly.

"Why are you such a bitch all of the time?" snapped Amanda.

She had been up all night and was exhausted, imagining every scenario possible and feeling like she should tell someone about the hand on the back incident from years ago.

"Shut up," replied Jackie as she continued to type. "Mom, why don't you get Dad's work laptop. Maybe you can log in to access his social media account while I do this."

Caroline agreed it was a good idea and headed down the hall to Greg's office. There, on his desk, was his slick, black work laptop. Gathering it up, she felt a moment of fear. What could be on this, or even the family laptop, that may give her the news of what could have happened to Greg and Noel?

Sitting back between the girls on the couch, she pulled open his laptop and was met with a screen to enter in a password. She didn't have a clue. "What do you think his password is?" she asked the girls.

They voiced out combinations of their names and birthdates. Caroline hesitated, scared that it may lock her out.

"Let's finish the post on my account and then worry about this," she said, closing the laptop.

"Okay, I'm done, and I'm going to post," Jackie said triumphantly.

Jackie was happy that she, again, did a better job at something compared to her sister. It didn't even matter that it was in regard to her missing family.

"Here, you can post this picture," Caroline said, texting it to Jackie to add to the post. A moment later Jackie hit "send" and the post went out to Caroline's social media network.

The post read:

Hi everyone, while I feel dread in writing this, I am seeking your help. My husband, Greg, has gone missing since Saturday, along with my dearest friend, Noel. I've reached out to the police without much help. Here's a photo of them taken on Saturday. If you know where they are, or have seen them, please message me. We are scared and unsure of their whereabouts. Thank you all.

A few moments later, the likes started and a few messages of condolences and concern about the situation appeared in the comments below the photo.

Caroline and the girls read over each one, hoping for an answer. But there was nothing of real use.

"Now what?" asked Caroline. In her mind, she thought the answer would have just appeared like everything else on the platform. But nothing of substance was posted.

"Now we just wait," answered Amanda. "But let's try Dad's account and see if we can get in to post there, too."

CHAPTER 26

MOUNT KATAHDIN, MAINE

Monday, May 10, at 8:17 a.m.

Officer Kelly, with the report from Dr. Isaac in hand, walked into the police station. He was going to investigate the area more that afternoon and had already been down by the lake that morning taking pictures and collecting additional evidence. He had cleared out the small conference room at the station to dedicate it solely to the investigation.

Sitting at the table in the conference room, he pulled open his laptop. His phone began to ring with an unknown number. It was another reporter looking for more details on the case. Reporters had been calling him nonstop. Officer Kelly was unsure of what to say to any of them, so he gave broad details with statements like, "We aren't yet ready to comment on this story," and then hung up.

He logged in to his computer then picked up his now silent phone and texted Chauncy, the administrator for the town who managed the social media for the few postings that the police, fire, and town shared. He wanted her to post something on social media about the victims but was unsure what to write.

He quickly perused the report and opened the notepad on his phone. He tried a few variations of a post, starting with something generic first about a man and a woman being found and requesting people to contact him if they were missing someone. But that felt too vague.

Meanwhile, Chauncy sent him the login name and password to the town's account. He put his phone down and logged in to the town's social media account in official capacity. Now it felt real. What on earth would he write?

Playing with words and phrases, nothing stuck. Officer Kelly picked up the report and began reading through it. A lot of the terminology was unfamiliar but he hoped something would jump out. There were a few Polaroid pictures that Dr. Isaac had taken of the bodies.

Officer Kelly was waiting for the sketches of their faces to be sent back from an artist in Portland. Dr. Isaac had noted in the file that he had taken a few pictures on his phone and texted them to an artist he knew there. In the notes, it said the artist would be sending the sketches directly to Officer Kelly.

Officer Kelly appreciated all the help that Dr. Isaac had given him. Things like this with photos weren't something that he thought about, so it was a step that he imagined would help, but he was still concerned about whether it would.

Stopping on one page of the report, he read through Dr. Isaac's comments about the tattoos on each of the parties. He had included a few Polaroids of each with a detailed description of the ink that decorated each person's body.

Maybe this could help, thought Officer Kelly.

He went back to his phone and began writing up a new description. Meanwhile, as he typed, his phone rang with more calls from reporters and then the sound of a text message. It, too, was a number he didn't recognize. Opening the message, the face of the dead man looked back at him. "Ding," another text. He opened it. There was the face of the woman. This was it. He had what he needed.

Logging back in to his laptop, the social media home page stared back at him, with 109 people who followed the account. Beginning his post, the words finally came to him:

On the afternoon of Sunday, May 14, two unidentified bodies were found near Mount Katahdin in Maine. One male and one female, ages 48–52. The female had several tattoos and the male had one. Please review the attached photos. If you know these people, please contact Officer Kelly at 207-678-9990. You will also be asked to identify the other tattoos to aid in ensuring calls are legitimate.

He hit "post." Now it was time to wait. He hoped that one of the 109 people who followed the account would have the answers about who these two people were.

A few minutes later, he refreshed the browser, hoping for some sort of response. Nothing. He refreshed it again. Nothing. He decided to get a cup of coffee.

When he came back, he refreshed it again. Marcus had put an emoji of a crying person in the comments. Refreshing again, there was another comment. His heart skipped a beat.

It was a local logger who was known to cause trouble at the town bar. Would it be this easy? Was Dr. Isaac clued into this, somehow knowing it could have been someone who knew how to use a chainsaw? Could this be the murderer?

Reading the comment, his heart sank: *You pigs are so dumb, you ain't never gonna figure this out.*

CHAPTER 27

MOUNT KATAHDIN, MAINE

Monday, May 10, at 8:21 a.m.

Marigold called out of work that Monday morning. She couldn't go in and face the reporters, crime scene tape, and questions. She had dropped the twins off at school and Marcus had come by in the morning to check on her. She didn't want to get out of bed. She didn't want to talk. She just wanted her mind to be blank.

Marigold had called Iris the night before when she got home to tell her about what had happened. She told her that something bad happened but didn't get into the details. Iris sounded surprised and asked if the children knew.

"Of course the kids know," Marigold told Iris. "I had to tell them."

"Ma," whined Iris. "They are children. They don't need to know about all the bad stuff like this in the world and right near 'em."

As Marigold lay in bed, she thought about her conversation with her daughter. Of course the children needed to know. They needed to know to stay safe and away from strangers.

She could hear Sammy in the background. It almost felt like he wouldn't leave Iris alone while they were talking. When Sammy was there, he always kept an eye on Iris, watching her every move. It drove Marigold crazy to think that maybe her daughter had a controlling boyfriend like that.

But over the weekend while they were visiting, he was acting weirder than usual to Marigold. He was out by himself a lot in the woods and didn't talk to either of the children. Iris seemed to be more attentive to the kids than usual, and it made Marigold happy to see their interactions for the limited time that she was home with them before her shift at the inn.

"Ma, who do they think the people are?" Iris had asked the night before.

Marigold told her she had no idea and it didn't seem like the cops did either.

"Who do they think did it?" Iris further inquired.

Marigold told her she had no clue and didn't think the police did either.

Marigold's mind switched from thinking about last night's conversation with her daughter to what she was going to do next. Could she even go back to the inn and work? Were people always going to ask her about it? Forever now, she'd be haunted with this.

Pulling herself out of bed, she wandered into the kitchen where a cold cup of coffee sat on the counter. Marcus had left it there when he popped in to check on her on his way to work.

Sitting herself down at the counter and taking a sip, she looked at her phone. There were a few numbers she didn't know and a call from Officer Kelly. She listened to the voicemail. It was Officer Kelly telling her he hoped she was doing okay and that he made a post on social media to try to figure out who the two people were.

She opened her social media app and was met with photos of Iris with the kids from the weekend, followed by the post from the town about the two bodies. As Marigold read the description, she wondered about the tattoos mentioned and what the unmentioned ones looked like. What were they and what did they mean to these people who were found dead in the woods of Maine?

Placing the phone back down on the counter, she took another sip of cold coffee. Maybe she could move and take the twins with her to start fresh someplace else. Maybe this was a sign from God that it was time to move on. She picked up her phone again and went back to the post on social media.

Re-reading the post, she noticed the drawings attached. Pulling the man's rendition up on her screen, she wondered if he was a kind man, a man who treated women well. Maybe he was married to the woman. She flipped to the woman's picture and shuddered, flashing back to opening the bag and seeing her hand.

Marigold made herself stare at the phone. "Who are you?" she asked. "Why are you here?" The woman stared back, silent. Marigold imagined what her voice sounded like. She wondered what the woman's tattoos were and the man's. She scrolled back to the man's picture, trying to remember if she had ever met him at the inn.

Maybe they had been married there and had come back annually for their anniversary and she just never noticed them because they were ordinary, quiet. But what happened to them was neither ordinary nor quiet.

As she read the post again, she noticed how much attention it was getting. It already had forty likes and several comments. Reading through, none were of any real substance, but a few were interesting. She thought of the families of these two people and what they must be thinking, not knowing where their beloveds were.

She put her phone down again. The images of their faces were behind her eyelids every time she closed them. Would they live there forever? Would she see their faces watching her for the rest of her life? She hoped not.

Propping herself up from the counter, she grabbed her cigarettes and headed to the front door to smoke on the porch. She pulled her black hair back into a ponytail.

The twins hated when she smoked in the house. They hated the smell. She did her best to smoke only outside. As she puffed, the birds sang and squirrels zipped around the yard. She paced from one side of the porch to the other and said a prayer for the two new residents now engrained forever in her mind.

CHAPTER 28

NEWBURYPORT, MASSACHUSETTS

Monday, May 10, at 9:22 a.m.

Caroline and her twins had been brainstorming potential passwords to their father's social media account. They had already locked themselves out of his work laptop and didn't want to disable his social media account on the family laptop, too.

His assistant, Monique, had called around 8:30 that morning, wondering if he was sick. Caroline took a deep breath and explained the situation. Monique was shocked and said she would pass the message along to Mr. Clark, Greg's boss.

Before hanging up, Caroline asked Monique if there was a way to log in to Greg's computer. She thought for a moment and then explained that Jose, the IT manager, was out that day, but he'd be the one who could look up Greg's password. Monique promised she'd ask Jose about the situation to see if they could access anything on his computer.

Caroline thanked her, hung up, and told the girls what Monique said. At that point, Jackie was still formulating passwords and Amanda was monitoring social media and replying to messages and comments. While many reached out, no one had information.

"Should I call Officer McKenna?" Caroline asked the girls.

"Yeah, Mom, I would," replied Jackie, not looking up from her list. Amanda nodded in agreement.

*　*　*　*　*

Maria picked up the ringing phone. She was greeted by Caroline, who reminded her of who she was and explained again about the situation. Maria's heart sank. Of course she remembered who Caroline was and what had happened. She couldn't shake it out of her mind.

That morning when she got to work, Maria confided in Officer McKenna that she had thought about Caroline all night long and hadn't slept wondering what had happened to her friend and husband. Officer McKenna, surprisingly cold, told her to get over it. He said the husband probably ran off with the friend and got in some kind of trouble or that they were in some cheap hotel room shacking up since he was sick of his wife's shit and daughters' attitudes.

Up to that point, Maria always considered Officer McKenna to be a friend. She could tell that he liked her. She'd catch him looking at her as she moved around the station. He always lingered a little too long by her at the front desk, trying to learn more about her life.

But now it was the next day and he had told the woman that her husband and friend would probably be home by this time. Maria was shocked that he had been wrong.

"Oh my God," Maria whispered over the line, losing her level of professionalism. "They still aren't back?"

Caroline could hear the genuine concern in her voice.

"No, they still aren't back," she told Maria. "Is that officer in? May I speak to him to launch a formal report?"

"Yes," said Maria and put Caroline on hold. She feared telling Officer McKenna but knew she had to push this. She had to help.

As she approached his desk, he looked up from his paper and donut. Normally he was excited to see Maria coming his way, but not today. He, too, couldn't get the missing people out of this head.

"She's on the phone again," Maria told him, and she could tell by his expression that he immediately knew who she was talking about. He looked away from her and then back, looking annoyed.

"Are you fucking kidding me?" he asked.

Maria stepped back, shocked at his tone and word choice. He knew that she didn't like swearing.

"Um, no," replied Maria. "What should I do?"

"Transfer her over to me," he told her and slammed his hand on the desk. "I'll take a formal report. I hope to God these people show up today. This is wasting my fucking time."

Maria scurried back to her desk and transferred the call to his line. She watched the red light on her phone indicating his line was in use. The call lasted for a few moments. She timed it with her phone. She hoped he was being kind every second. When the call ended, he walked past her and out the door without saying a word.

Maria didn't know what Officer McKenna was going to do. But later that morning when he arrived back, he briefly told her that he visited the house again and examined a scratch on the wall without finding much out. He told Maria that the women had posted something on social media, and he had written up a formal report while he was there. He then stormed back to his desk. She wondered where his frustration was coming from. One time, he told her that his father cheated and left him and his mother. She wondered if this fueled it somehow.

While Officer McKenna was busy, Maria snuck her phone onto her lap and opened her social media account. She typed in Caroline's name and there she was. A beautiful picture of her with a dog and a man next to her. Both were smiling. Scrolling down, she saw the post asking if people had seen her husband

and friend. Maria looked at the photo Caroline had uploaded, the husband and friend smiling up at her.

Venturing back to Caroline's profile, she read the comments from people expressing their condolences and offering to help in whatever way they could. She read the responses from what she assumed were Caroline's two daughters.

Deciding that she, too, wanted to help, she liked the post and then shared it on her profile, making the comment, "Please help the family find their loved ones" and adding a heart emoji.

CHAPTER 29

NORTH END, BOSTON, MASSACHUSETTS

Greg and Caroline, twenty-eight years ago

When Greg asked Caroline to marry him, it was anything but romantically spectacular, and nothing like what you see in the movies. They were still living in Boston in his aunt's apartment. It was a Saturday night in November. The leaves had fallen in the Common and the air had a particularly cold sting in it. It wasn't quite the feel of winter, but it was stronger than the usual fall temperatures for New England.

Caroline had spent her late afternoon wandering around the shops in the neighborhood and got a coffee around the corner from the apartment. She sat wrapped in a scarf drinking her coffee on their front stairs. She wore thin sunglasses and her hair was nestled on top of her head with an elastic band.

Coming down the street was a man. He was handsome and familiar. She smiled. As he began to pass, he stopped.

"Excuse me, miss," he said. "Are you alone?"

"I am," she replied and motioned for him to sit down. He did and reached for her coffee, pulling it toward his lips.

"That's awfully familiar of you," she said and transitioned her sunglasses from her eyes to the top of her head.

"Ah, it is," he said and smacked his lips.

She liked when Greg did things like this. It made their relationship feel new and fun again.

"Want to go home?" he asked.

She nodded and the two got up. She twined her arm through his and they walked up the stairs.

A little while later, he poured her a glass of wine and she settled in the living room with her notepad to write. A few hours later, he asked her if she wanted to venture out to the North End for dinner.

"Can't we just get takeout?" she asked, not wanting to leave the house or change into something dressier.

"No, come on," he tempted. "It will be fun."

She finally agreed. Greg told her she didn't need to change and could go as she was. She gave in to his argument and the two stepped out into the chilly Boston night. They picked a place on the corner. Caroline could never remember the name, but they had eaten there before. She liked it, and he did, too. That night, Greg ordered an expensive bottle of red wine.

"Big first date?" she teased.

The two had come there on their first date night in Boston. At that time, they didn't have any money to speak of, but Greg's aunt had slipped them some cash to get a good meal in the city. When they sat down, they whispered back and forth deciding if they could afford a bottle of wine to split. Luckily, to their surprise, an older couple next to them left, leaving a half full bottle on the table. Greg glanced around the restaurant then reached for the bottle, welcoming it to their table.

Caroline was shocked and whispered sternly how rude that was for him to do. He shrugged and told her it was fine. His effort didn't go unnoticed. The waitress came back with two glasses and winked. "I would have done the same thing," she said.

But now they could afford their own bottle. This one was more expensive than what Caroline would have liked to pay, but she let it slide. She was already out of the house in a less-than-desirable outfit, so at least the bottle of wine would let the server know they weren't poor and homeless.

Over dinner, they talked about work and Greg's aunt. Caroline could feel the wine going to her head and her cheeks. Greg kept up the conversation and she was surprised at how talkative he was—more than usual. When the waitress asked if they wanted dessert in the now almost empty restaurant, Caroline shook her head no. But Greg said they did and asked for tiramisu.

Caroline was surprised because he never wanted anything sweet. She never did either.

"Come on, live a little," he told her.

The dessert came with two spoons and the two dipped into the ladyfingers. Putting their spoons down a few moments later, they locked eyes. Caroline felt like something was wrong. She suddenly thought he was going to break up with her right then and there.

Instead, he began shuffling his hands around in this coat.

"What are you doing?" she asked, wanting to get past this awkward moment.

To her surprise, he stood up from the table and then bent down. Caroline looked at the floor wondering if he had dropped money or the credit card. They were now eye to eye and to her shock, he was on one knee. Behind him, the waitress and kitchen staff watched from the counter.

"Caroline," he began. "I've loved you for a very long time now. And it would be my great honor and privilege to have you as my wife. Will you marry me?"

Greg then pulled out the ring box and opened it with both hands. There, against a black velvet backdrop was a sparkling pear-shaped diamond. Caroline stared at it not knowing what to say. She and Greg had talked about this moment, but she thought it was going to look different and feel different. But here they were in the North End, on a crisp November evening, and she was getting proposed to.

She reached for the ring, but Greg beat her to it, pulling it from the confines of velvet. Reaching for her hand, he slid it on.

Caroline pulled her hand to her face admiring the large stone. The ring was perfect, like Greg. But in a way, it didn't totally feel like her as she admired it on her finger.

Caroline loved him and it felt like it was the right time to get married. It was time to say yes. It was time to move on from Matt and from college. It was time to be an adult and move forward with life with someone who offered so much.

"Well?" he asked. "Don't keep me hanging."

"Yes," she finally choked out. "Yes, Greg, I will marry you."

Then they heard applause jolting them back into the moment. Greg got up, turned around, and waved to the staff. He then reached down to pull Caroline up toward him. Knowing that they had to look the part, he leaned in for a kiss. But she moved her head as he did, making his front teeth hit her cheek.

Their lips finally met and they kissed, then looked back at the restaurant staff. Greg threw some money on the table and the two took off into the night back toward the apartment and to plan the next chapter of their life together.

CHAPTER 30

MOUNT KATAHDIN, MAINE

Monday, May 10, at 10:01 a.m.

Officer Kelly decided he needed to understand the scene of the crime more. He was consumed with wondering who these two people were and how their lives ended so tragically. He had been keeping an eye on the social media comments and shares to see if any loggers or tree cutters seemed suspicious, to Dr. Isaac's point.

On his way back to the crime scene, he stopped at the logger's shack who had made the comments about the police being pigs. Maybe this guy knew something, or maybe he was just an asshole. Officer Kelly didn't want to make any mistakes, so he stopped near the shack. Gus, the owner and commenter, was out in the front yard cleaning his gun.

"Hey pig," he said when Officer Kelly arrived.

"Gus, where have you been the last few days?" Officer Kelly asked, ignoring the comment.

"Right the damn here," replied Gus.

Gus was hard. Tattooed. Bearded. He was born there, had grown up there, and would die there. He'd transport trees all over the East Coast but never wanted to be anywhere else but here.

"You got anything to do with these murders?" asked Officer Kelly.

He knew that Gus did petty things and even beat up a few guys here and there, but maybe something happened out on one of his runs and his petty crimes turned out to be more serious.

"Are you fucking kidding me? Man, I knew you guys were all dumb working down there at that old station arresting tourists for throwing out empties on these roads, but not this dumb," replied Gus and he placed down his gun. "You got a warrant? You got anything else to say?"

Officer Kelly eyed the yard. Nothing looked out of place. "Okay then," he said and got in the cruiser to head up to the lake.

There were still a few officers milling around the crime scene that was covered in yellow tape like a bad wrapping job on a Christmas gift. Officer Kelly ducked below it, greeting the officers, who were both local and from out of town.

"Find anything?" he asked one young officer.

He shook his head. Officer Kelly began walking toward where the top half of the woman's body had been. Scanning the ground, he saw leaves and dirt, sticks and some rocks. There was no blood since she had been wrapped so tightly within the trash bag.

He circled around where she had been placed. Still nothing. It was like she had fallen from the sky. Officer Kelly then began the short walk up the street to where her bottom half and the man had been found. Taking his time, he examined the ditch that ran parallel to the road. Nothing.

Inspecting the tree that the man had been found near, he noticed a scratch mark in the bark. Was this related or just a random mark? Crouching down again, he looked all throughout the grass where the man's body had been. The grass was scrunched down due to the man's weight, but nothing else looked suspicious.

Officer Kelly then stepped to where the woman's lower half had been found. Still nothing. Deciding this wasn't sufficient, he made his way back to the road and began walking in the direction of the mountain. His eyes darted from side to side hoping something on either side of the road would pop out. Nothing did.

The grass was high with the spring rainfall. It was thick, too, making it difficult to see anything abnormal. He walked up and down that road a few times before deciding to give himself a break and head back to the station. Maybe a clue came in or someone saw the post and the renditions, and things would start to move.

Arriving at the station, he greeted Chauncy and headed to the small conference room. Opening up the laptop, he scanned the comments. Nothing of substance, just people expressing their concern. A few tourists had seen the post and were asking questions in the comments about whether it was safe to visit the area if there was a madman on the loose killing people.

Officer Kelly ignored those comments, as locals were still encouraging the out-of-towners to come. They wanted the tourist dollars and having any lag in visitor traffic would be disastrous for the area businesses. Frustrated, Officer Kelly logged out of the town account and into his own.

Searching for the town name, he pulled up the profile and shared the post about the bodies on his own profile. Maybe a buddy or friend from the academy would see it and be able to offer information. He'd take anything at this point.

He wondered if he should call Dr. Isaac but decided against it. There was nothing else Dr. Isaac could help him with now. By this point, it was almost noon. He was hungry and tired. Sleep wouldn't be an option but going to the local pizza shop to get a sandwich would be. He needed the energy and the comfort of something good in his stomach to help him get through the afternoon.

Driving to the pizza place, he wondered when an answer would come. Would it be today? Would it be tomorrow? He took a deep breath and said a prayer to himself, hoping that it would come sooner than later.

CHAPTER 31

NEWBURYPORT, MASSACHUSETTS

Monday, May 10, at 11:59 a.m.

"**M**om, so many people are saying that they haven't seen Dad or Noel," stated Amanda.

She said it without emotion. It was a fact and she couldn't quite bring herself to internalize what she was actually saying. Her mother and Jackie looked up at her from their perches at the table.

Monique had called about an hour ago. She had asked Jose to reset the password and after that, Caroline was able to log in to the laptop. Monique had debated about getting her the access but thought it was the right thing to do. Jose swore he wouldn't tell anyone due to the circumstances.

Caroline had searched through Greg's work emails and calendar holds. Nothing seemed out of the ordinary. Curiosity had gotten the best of her and she did scroll back a few years to that time Greg hadn't come home that weekend and said he was staying in Georgia. But the only hold on his calendar for that weekend was "Golf with John Smith and associates." That was it. Nothing, absolutely nothing.

When she tried his social media account on the work laptop, she wasn't able to log in. He hadn't saved his password. Jackie was on the family laptop trying different password variations and trying to contact the social media help desk about this emergency situation to see if she could get the account unlocked.

Amanda was on her own social media account posting and following up with those who commented between public posts and direct messages. No one knew anything.

The three women were frustrated and hungry. If Noel had been there and they had been looking for Greg, she would have been the one to run out to the store and bring home armloads of groceries to make a meal. But there was no Noel. Caroline had ventured over to the neighbor's house that morning and told them about the situation.

Molly and Frank were surprised to hear the news.

"You mean, when we saw you on Saturday and you said that they were gone, they never came back?" asked Molly.

Caroline told her yes and Molly offered to help. Throughout the morning, Molly had popped in and out. At 11:30 a.m., she stopped in and brought them lunch.

"Hello everyone," chirped Molly. In her hands were a plate towering with sandwiches and a bag of chips. "Who's hungry and needs a break?"

Molly set the sandwiches on the counter.

"What kind?" asked Jackie.

"Ham salad, tuna salad, and egg salad," Molly answered.

Jackie looked at Amanda and winced. Caroline saw her face and kicked her under the table.

"Thank you, Molly. This is incredibly kind of you," said Caroline.

The girls chimed in, thanking her, too. Molly turned from the counter to the three women.

"Any luck finding them?" Molly asked.

"No," the three replied in unison.

Caroline reached back and selected a tuna salad sandwich. A piece of tuna fell to the floor.

Molly gasped. "Oh no! Let me fix you a plate," she said and moved to the kitchen, grabbing plates out of the cabinet.

As she began to fix plates for the women, their eyes fixated back to their specific screens, hoping that maybe an answer had come. Jackie noticed that a woman named Maria had liked the post. She wasn't sure who she was at first but realized the connection when she clicked on the woman's name. It was Maria from the police station.

Amanda began scrolling again. She had gone to college in Maine and had friends who still lived there. One of them had commented on a post that caught her eye. It was about two people who were found dead. The post didn't say too much about how they died. It sounded like they were murdered.

Amanda saw Molly place a plate next to the computer and she could hear the murmur of her mother and sister talking. She re-read the post to herself:

On the afternoon of Sunday, May 14, two unidentified bodies were found near Mount Katahdin in Maine. One male and one female, ages 48–52. The female had several tattoos and the male had one. Please review the attached photos. If you know these people, please contact Officer Kelly at 207-678-9990. You will also be asked to identify the other tattoos to aid in ensuring calls are legitimate.

After reading, she clicked on the two attached photos and gasped. A face somewhat resembling her father's looked back at her. Caroline, Molly, and Jackie stopped talking and chewing and looked at her.

"Amanda, what's wrong?" Caroline asked.

Amanda put her hands up to her face and began shaking her head uncontrollably.

"Amanda, what is wrong?" Caroline asked, starting to feel sick.

Jackie looked from her mother to her sister and then back again. "What's going on?" she asked.

"Mom," croaked Amanda, starting to point at the screen.

Caroline jumped up and moved behind her daughter trying to see what she saw. There, looking up at her, was a face that kind of looked like Greg. But the face looked fatter. Jackie followed suit. Her mouth dropped.

"Oh my God," Jackie said.

"Amanda, what did the post say?" asked Caroline.

Amanda kept shaking her head no. She couldn't believe what she had read, let alone tell her mother. Caroline pushed Amanda from the chair to get to the laptop. She tried to close out the photo but hit the wrong part of the touchpad on the laptop and instead advanced to the next photo. There, staring back at all three, was a face that almost looked like Noel.

The three all gasped. Molly stood at the door unsure of what to do. Jackie started to cry, trying to comprehend what she was looking at. Caroline froze. This couldn't be right.

"Amanda, get the post back," Caroline yelled. She knew it wasn't good, but maybe this was a mistake. Amanda's shaking hand reached toward the laptop to close out the photos, revealing the initial post.

The three began to read. Jackie's eyes filled up with even more tears. Amanda started shaking. Caroline's face turned white and she felt faint. This couldn't be true. This couldn't be her people. This had to be someone else's friends or family. She leaned in closer to the computer and re-read the post. Everything stopped. A ringing filled her ears. Tears began to fill her eyes.

Molly, realizing something happened, told the three she'd go call the police. She turned and no one noticed her red hair bobbing quickly across the lawn to her own home. None of them heard her; they were too focused on the post.

"Mom, do you think this is Dad? And Noel?" asked Jackie.

Caroline began gasping for air and for words.

"I don't know," she whispered. "I just don't know. How did you see this? Is this some sort of joke?" asked Caroline.

Amanda began to cry, unable to speak.

"Where did you see this?" Caroline demanded.

Amanda still didn't answer. Caroline re-read the post. Could this really be her husband? Could this really be her friend? She leaned in closer to the laptop, studying the face of the man and then clicking to the photo of the woman. As the girls hugged each other, Caroline leaned back trying to get a new angle on the photo. As the faces stared back at her, she heard sirens shrieking in the distance.

CHAPTER 32

MOUNT KATAHDIN, MAINE

Monday, May 10, at 2:00 p.m.

Officer Kelly's cell phone rang. It was another unknown number. He was sitting in the conference room, reading over the medical report and his own notes from the crime scene again. He'd take a break every thirty minutes or so to refresh his coffee and check social media.

The number called again. He ignored it. Then again. He decided to answer.

"Hello, Officer Tommy Kelly," he said.

"Hello, Officer Kelly," said the voice. "My name is Officer Luke McKenna. I live in Massachusetts. I'm calling because I have some questions about the social media post you shared about the two bodies you found. I may have some information."

Officer Kelly's heart skipped a beat. At the same time, he heard his phone vibrate and looked quickly.

"Yes, sir," Officer Kelly replied. "I'd like to hear more."

"I have a woman and her two daughters down here in Newburyport saying that their father and family friend randomly disappeared late Saturday afternoon. They haven't been seen since," he explained. "They somehow saw the pictures on social media and think that these may be the people they're looking for."

Officer Kelly was shocked. He thought that it would take a few days—maybe even a few weeks—for the people in the photos to be identified. He had hoped that it would be quick, but never did he think it would be this quick.

"Can you tell me more about the bodies?" asked Officer McKenna.

Caroline and the girls had shared some information between gasps and tears when Officer McKenna arrived at the house after the neighbor's call. He'd never seen people cry like this before. Even the dog seemed sad, as if she knew something terrible had happened.

Officer Kelly sighed. He hated to get into detail and didn't want to share too much in case there was any misunderstanding with the people in the sketches.

"One of the bodies wasn't in great shape," he began.

"How so?" asked Officer McKenna, confused by the statement. He assumed that since the faces in the drawings looked decent, it was probably death by gunshot for a clean kill.

"Well," began Officer Kelly, "one died from a gunshot to the head. The man."

"What about the other one?" Officer McKenna asked. "The woman?"

Officer Kelly took a deep breath and paused. "She was strangled," he replied. "And cut in half. We think with a chainsaw."

"A what?" Officer McKenna managed to say after a few moments. "Cut in half? By a chainsaw? Are you fucking kidding me? I don't get paid enough to deal with this type of shit."

"Yes," answered Officer Kelly, unsure of what else to say to Officer McKenna's response. Then it occurred to him. "What are their names?" he asked. He still wasn't sure if it was a direct match but hoped it was to help solve the case.

"The man is Greg Montgomery," said Officer McKenna. "The woman is Noel Clark."

"Noel, like Christmas?" asked Officer Kelly.

"Yes, Noel like Christmas," replied Officer McKenna. "Can you confirm any of the identifying tattoos?"

"The man has a bird tattoo on his butt cheek. Does your victim?" asked Officer McKenna.

"Yes," replied Officer Kelly, yet again met with mixed emotion about identifying the pair.

"I haven't worked on very many crimes like this," admitted Officer McKenna. Officer Kelly stated the same.

"Let me talk to the family and see if we can get them up there to identify the bodies," said Officer McKenna. "I'll talk to a few people here at my station and then go over to the family's house again. In the meantime, I'll try and keep this quiet on my end until we know for sure."

* * * * *

Officer McKenna placed his cell phone down. Looking up, he saw Maria gazing at him with a concerned look on her face.

"I think we have a match. But this is some fucked shit," he said and got up from his desk to tell the police chief.

Twenty minutes later, Officer McKenna was in his car and headed back to Caroline's house. It was up to him to tell the family that it may be a match and for him to convince them to drive the five hours up to Maine to identify the bodies.

Pulling in the driveway, he saw the curtains were drawn and no one was in the yard, similar to his first few times coming here. The house looked sad. He got out of the car and walked to the door, where he was met by Amanda, who greeted him amid her tears.

"Come in," she said, motioning with her hand for him to enter.

He followed her into the kitchen where Caroline, Jackie, and Rose were. Caroline was still pale and Jackie's face was red from wiping tears.

"I didn't think I'd see you back here so soon," said Caroline, trying to smile. "Do we have the wrong people?"

She hoped he'd say yes and that the tattoos she explained to him weren't on the dead people in Maine. Amanda knew about Noel's secret tattoo but failed to tell Officer McKenna. She feared that if this was all some huge misunderstanding it would ruin their relationship moving forward.

"I'm afraid the man has a tattoo matching the description you gave me," he said, trying to take the chief's advice of being factual and to the point.

The three women looked at him with horror in their eyes.

"I'm afraid it gets worse," he said. "I think we're going to need you to head up there and identify the bodies."

"The man's name is Greg and he's my father," snapped Jackie, suddenly feeling angry at the coldness from Officer McKenna.

"Yes, miss, I know," he responded, sensing her frustration. "I can't help make arrangements for you to get up there but a guy up there should be able to help. His name is Officer Kelly."

"Officer Kelly?" asked Amanda. "He's handling the case?"

"I'm not sure," replied Officer McKenna. "We didn't get into that much detail. Sounds like he's the guy in charge. We only talked briefly."

"When do we need to go?" asked Caroline, trying to get the conversation refocused. "Should I start packing? Should someone stay here in case it's not them and they come back?"

"You should probably start heading up as soon as you can," said Officer McKenna. "I'd say pack for a day or two. Can one of you stay behind? In case someone comes back or shows up with information about them?"

"I think we both want to go with our mom," said Amanda.

Tears began to build in her eyes again. Jackie nodded in agreement.

"Understood," said Officer McKenna. "I'll have someone come and park here at the house while you're gone just in case. Somebody down at the station should have the time."

"Thank you," said Caroline. "I'll see if the neighbors can keep an eye on the place, too. And Rose. It's probably too much to bring her."

"I'll call up to Maine and let them know you're coming. At this point, you probably won't get up there until eight thirty or so this evening," stated Officer McKenna.

Caroline trembled. The idea of having to identify the bodies of two people she loved so much was hard to comprehend. How was this happening to her and her family? She put her hand down on the table to steady herself.

"I think we'll go up tonight and see how we feel when we get there," Caroline said. She couldn't make that decision in the moment.

"How will we get up there?" asked Jackie. "It's such a long drive."

"We'll just split the driving up," said Amanda.

Caroline had begun to walk across the kitchen toward the living room, trying to make her way up the stairs to start packing.

"I would say," said Officer McKenna, noticing her nervousness, "give thought and take notes on who may want to hurt either of these people. And make notes about anything else you think I should know about either of them, their lives. Anything like affairs, bad work relationships, debts, or anything similar."

"Affairs? Bad relationships?" asked Caroline.

"Debts?" asked Jackie immediately after.

"Yes," confirmed Officer McKenna. "We're going to need all the clues we can get. It doesn't sound like they have much information in Maine. Please call down to the station once you identify the bodies."

Officer McKenna tipped his hat and headed to the door. He hoped he would never have to come back there again.

CHAPTER 33

NEWBURYPORT, MASSACHUSETTS

Monday, May 10, at 3:21 p.m.

The girls packed the car as quickly as they could. Unsure of what to bring, they both ran around the house throwing clothes and food into laundry baskets. This was their father's trick to pack for road trips by putting clothes in a laundry basket. That way, you get to where you are going, unpack, and then when things are dirty, you place them back in the basket so that when everyone gets home, it's as easy as dropping everything in the washing machine.

Caroline preferred packing. She thought the car looked cluttered when there were laundry baskets stacked on top of one another. What if people thought they were homeless? But she also figured that wouldn't be the case, seeing that they had upgraded their SUVs over the years, recently to the latest model BMW.

But now here were the girls racing to pack like their father while she felt like she was moving around the house through invisible cement. Everything felt hard to do. Time wasn't moving. Life as she knew it was moving in slow motion. Rose, though, stayed by her side as she meandered through the house. The girls, who could apparently tell she was having a hard time, gave her the task of making some sandwiches for the ride to add to the ones that Molly had made.

But the bread was frozen. She had meant to take it out Saturday night to make sandwiches for a Sunday picnic that she, Greg, and Noel had planned at the island. She always froze the bread in an attempt to avoid carbs to stay thin and make it harder to eat readily. Noel had laughed at her about this ever since they were in their thirties.

"How can you not eat bread?" Noel had asked.

It wasn't the first time she had asked her, but on that particular cold February morning in Boston, Caroline had questioned it herself. Caroline's girls were in their second year of college and Noel was up for the weekend to attend some event at the Museum of Fine Arts.

They had decided to meet for brunch in Back Bay. Noel had been a few minutes late but Caroline didn't mind. She had ordered a black coffee and was sipping it when her friend tore into the place full of apologies.

Caroline couldn't remember what else they had talked about that day. But she remembered how good the bread had looked. Noel, grabbing for the bread basket and smears she had ordered, fixed Caroline a plate with a small muffin, a crusty chunk of Italian bread, and a baby croissant. On the side, she had plastered fresh strawberry jam, freshly whipped cream, and a slab of butter.

"Eat," she had told Caroline, and she lifted her bread up like it was a glass she was saying cheers with.

Caroline smiled and looked at the plate. Picking up the small muffin, she bit the top off.

"The best part," said Noel.

Caroline remembered biting into the muffin and immediately wishing she had chosen the bread instead of wasting calories on a muffin that wasn't very good.

"Mom, how are you doing with the sandwiches?" asked Amanda, as she jetted by with a clothes basket, jolting Caroline from her memory.

Caroline nodded but wasn't quite sure what to do with the frozen bread.

"Just put it in the microwave and warm it up," said Jackie, coming up from behind her sister.

Caroline did as she was told while she tried to comprehend the whole situation. She was making sandwiches for a drive to God-knows-where Maine to identify the bodies of her husband and her friend. The thought struck her, chills ran down her back, and she began to cry again.

Not wanting the girls to see her, she shuffled down the hall to Greg's office. Closing the door, she sat at his desk and looked at his laptop that one of the girls had put back. She and the girls had given up trying to find any clues there. Jose had been helpful, yet no matter what they did they were unable to figure out Greg's social media password.

Sitting at the desk, Caroline put her head in her hands and let her tears pour onto the monogrammed leather desk blotter. She could hear that the girls were back in the house and running back up the stairs. Caroline knew it would be time to go soon and she'd have to get herself together.

Lifting her head up, she dropped her hands to her lap. Not even realizing it, she lifted one hand and then the other up under the desk and ran her fingers along the bottom of the top desk drawer.

The wood felt smooth, comforting. She ran her fingers back and forth. And then they stopped. There, under the desk, she felt something. She tried pulling it but nothing happened, so she got on her knees and crouched under the desk. And there, she saw it. A folded yellow piece of paper taped to the bottom of the drawer.

Her heart sank. Her stomach felt sick.

"Mom, are you ready?" yelled Jackie.

Caroline was torn on what to do.

"Almost," she yelled back in a hoarse voice.

Looking at the paper, she debated about whether or not to open the note. What if it was a clue? What if it was something else?

"Mom? Are you okay? Ready to go?" asked Amanda.

"Yes, honey," Caroline answered, realizing that now wasn't the time to open the piece of paper.

Caroline opened the top desk drawer and slipped the note in.

CHAPTER 34

MOUNT KATAHDIN, MAINE

Monday, May 10, at 3:43 p.m.

Officer Kelly got word from the officer in Massachusetts that three women were on their way to identify the bodies. He was surprised that they were coming up so late in the day.

He was sitting in his makeshift office reviewing the medical files, the photos from the crime scene, and the notes from the interviews that he and the other officers had taken. None of it made sense.

Now getting news that the family of the victims were on their way, he was unsure what to do next. What would he say to these people? What would they be like? Would they be angry at him? What questions would they ask? And would he have answers?

The others at the station were helpful in trying to analyze what they knew. Earlier in the day, the team held a brainstorming session trying to figure out what had happened. They even conferenced in specialists from Portland and Boston to examine the evidence.

When he shared the information that three family members were on the way, the team and extended team agreed that Officer Kelly should be there to talk with them and that a backup officer should be there to help out.

He'd take the lead on interviewing them and was excited about that. This was his chance to prove himself.

To prepare, Officer Kelly decided he needed to talk to someone who could help him. Picking up his cell phone, he entered his password and ran his finger through his contacts. After scrolling up and down for a moment, he found the name he was looking for. Tapping it, the phone began to ring.

A few rings in, the voice answered. "Hello?"

"Hello there, Dr. Isaac," said Officer Kelly. "I hope you are doing good."

"Who is this?" inquired Dr. Isaac.

"It's Officer Kelly from a few days ago. You helped me with those two bodies," he answered.

There was a pause.

"Hello, son. How's it going? I'm surprised to be hearing from you so soon. Any leads?" inquired Dr. Isaac.

"Yes sir," said Officer Kelly. "I took your advice and put a lot of info up on social media and it looks like that helped to drum up some information."

Dr. Isaac laughed. "What did we ever do before social media?" he asked. "So, what's the story then? Drugs or bad timing or what?"

"Not sure yet, doctor," said Officer Kelly. "But a family is coming up to identify the bodies. From what I know, the woman's husband and friend went missing Saturday afternoon. She's coming with her two daughters."

"Well, this could be it, son," Dr. Isaac said. "Are you prepared to talk to them?"

Officer Kelly sighed. "That's where I'm struggling," he said. "I'm wondering if you can come back up. I know it's a drive for you, but what if they have questions that I can't answer? I think you being here may help," he said.

Dr. Isaac sighed. He felt bad for Officer Kelly and knew this situation was above the young man's expertise.

"When are they going to be there?" Dr. Isaac asked.

"In a few hours. They are coming up from Massachusetts near the New Hampshire state line. I'm thinking they'll be here around 8:30," said Officer Kelly.

"I'm on my way," Dr. Isaac said and hung up.

"Where are you going?" asked Pam. "Not back up to no-man's land, I hope? But I sense you are from the call."

"You were listening?" he asked, knowing the answer. She always listened.

Pam nodded with her hands on her apron-dressed hips.

"It should be quick. I'll be home tomorrow," he said.

"At this point, I may begin to suspect you're having an affair," she said as she turned back to making dinner, now for one, in the kitchen.

Twenty minutes later, he was in the car making his way back to the mountain.

CHAPTER 35

SOMEWHERE IN MAINE ON I-95 NORTH

Monday, May 10, at 5:03 p.m.

❝**R**emember when Dad used to tell us stories about how he and Mom met?" asked Amanda as Jackie twisted her car through traffic up Route 95.

"Yeah, I used to think it was super gross," replied Jackie.

Amanda hit her from the passenger's seat.

"Dad loved Mom so much," said Jackie.

Caroline was half paying attention. She was on her cell phone scrolling through social media reading the comments on the posts. People seemed genuinely concerned, and she was trying to show her appreciation by responding to every comment. It was exhausting, but she needed to keep her mind distracted. If not, she would think about what she was on her way to do.

In the car, she had made a few calls, first to Noel's parents, sister, and friends. Those were difficult conversations to have, and she ended up passing the phone to Amanda to explain. She also had Amanda call Greg's parents. They were going to pass the word on to his brothers.

Caroline lost her parents a few years back. Her mother died of cancer and then only months later her father died, too. There was no specific reason, but the doctor thought it was due to loneliness. They had been together for more than fifty years and they loved each other. It was the type of love and the type of deep affection that Caroline had always wanted and had searched for in those college years, first with Matt and then with Greg.

While Greg had always been affectionate and doted on Caroline, she never was able to fully be the same with him. A part of her always held back, not letting herself love him the way he loved her.

As the girls talked about the past and memories of their father and Noel, Caroline popped in her earbuds and began to play Neil Diamond, trying to relax. She wished she had brought wine for the ride but knew showing up under the influence wasn't the look she was trying for. She wasn't sure what type of look to put on, but she knew wine drunk wasn't a good choice.

As Neil sang, she began entering notes and questions into her phone. She wanted to be prepared with the right questions and information. She didn't want to forget anything. Her fingers sprinted over the keyboard, filling the notepad. Soon, she had to scroll back to refresh herself on what she had written.

She made an entry about finding the folded note under the desk and the inability to figure out the social media password. Were those things connected? She then made a note about the last-minute work trips and extended stays. The girls kept talking and Neil kept singing. She shut her eyes.

Caroline wondered what their last thoughts were. Were they about her or their relationship? The times they shared drinks over the years and the meals? Did they think about the children? She began to cry. Wiping the tears from her eyes, she thought about happier moments, like when she got Rose and when the girls graduated from college.

An hour went by and then another and another. Jackie drove the whole way following the quiet directions of the GPS voice.

"Where are we?" Amanda kept asking, getting more and more concerned about the location. "Do you think these people really could be Dad and Noel? Like really?"

Amanda wanted to talk about it more and what was to come, but Jackie wasn't interested.

"Service is starting to go in and out," said Jackie. "I don't think we have much farther to go. Maybe like ten minutes. Should we wake Mom?"

"No, let her sleep until we get there. How do you think she's going to be? Should we go in with her or wait outside?" asked Amanda.

"Who knows?" said Jackie. "This is insane."

Moments later, pulling into the hospital parking lot, Jackie stopped the car.

"Is this it?" she asked, surprised at how small it was.

"I think so," replied Amanda looking around.

Amanda reached her hand back and placed it on her mother's knee, gently rocking it to wake her. "Mom, we're here," she said.

Her mother's eyes fluttered as she tried to remember where she was and why. Then it struck her and she felt sick.

"Are we here?" asked Caroline.

"I think so," replied Amanda. "Is that a cop car?"

The three looked at an old police car parked next to the entrance. They could make out the profile of a man inside it. Jackie parked the car, and the three got out.

"Hi there," said the man, who had exited the cruiser. He paused. "Are you here for the..."

"Yes, we are," said Caroline, approaching the man. "My name is Caroline and these are my two daughters, Jackie and Amanda." She reached out to shake the man's hand.

"Nice to meet you, ma'am," he replied. "My name is Officer Kelly. Would you mind following me this way?"

Caroline took a breath and motioned to the girls to stay put. She didn't want them to see anything they didn't need to. She'd do this alone.

CHAPTER 36

MOUNT KATAHDIN, MAINE

Monday, May 10, at 8:16 p.m.

O fficer Kelly led the way down the white, musty-smelling halls. Caroline's heart raced. One time in college, Noel drank too much and had to be hospitalized. This felt like that, but she realized that her friend wouldn't be coming back out this time if it was her.

"How was the drive here?" Officer Kelly asked, glancing back at her.

"It was fine. Thank you," Caroline replied.

"I secured you and your family a room at a local inn for the night. I had them hold it a few extra days just in case," he said.

"That was kind of you," she replied.

He stopped in front of a white door.

"Um, ma'am, this is where the bodies are. I have the doctor who examined them on his way in case you do have questions," said Officer Kelly.

He wished that Dr. Isaac was already there by now. He wanted to avoid this alone time and awkwardness with her. But looking at her face now and seeing her concern, he realized she was just as scared as he was.

A nurse was walking down the hall toward them. They both looked in her direction. She walked over to the door without saying anything and unlocked it, then turned, nodded at them both, and continued down the hall.

Officer Kelly pushed open the unlocked door and stepped through. His hand wandered the wall looking for the light switch. The nurse had taught him how to open the vaults where the bodies were kept so he could pull each one out and examine it when he needed to.

Officer Kelly fumbled with the switches for a second and finally turned the light on. Caroline stepped through the door. The room was cold and smelled like cleaning solution. It was just like what she saw in the movies and on TV when people looked at bodies, but she was surprised to be seeing it in real life. She shivered.

"Are you cold?" asked Officer Kelly, noticing.

"Oh no, I'm fine. Thank you. Let's just get this done. What do we do now?" Caroline asked.

Officer Kelly nodded. He couldn't imagine how she must be feeling. She seemed like a nice enough woman. He wondered why she wasn't crying. Her blue eyes were puffy, and he figured there may be no tears left.

"Who do you want to see first?" he then asked.

Caroline's mouth dropped. She wasn't prepared to choose. Regardless of her choice, she knew if she saw one, she'd know the other was dead, too.

"Oh, um," she began. "I...I...don't know."

Caroline felt faint. Officer Kelly noticed her sway and rushed to get her a chair.

"Here, sit down," he said.

She followed his orders.

"I'll get you some water, too." He moved to the sink to grab a small cup and fill it with tap water.

Caroline shook her head, trying to get a grasp. Officer Kelly handed her the water. She took a sip.

"I'm sorry," Caroline said. "I'm not sure who to choose."

"I understand," replied Officer Kelly. "Why don't we sit for a few and then you can pick?"

He was hoping that Dr. Isaac would arrive momentarily and he could excuse himself out of the room.

"Should I get one of your daughters, or both?" he asked.

Caroline shook her head no. She was determined to do this herself. Her girls didn't need to have this memory ingrained in their minds for the rest of their lives. At that moment, the door opened. Officer Kelly turned to look and was elated.

"Hello there," said Dr. Isaac from the doorway. "I'm Dr. Isaac."

He moved toward Caroline and bent to shake her hand. "I've been helping this young man with the investigation. Have you identified the bodies yet?"

"No," replied Caroline.

"Well, okay then," he said. "Ma'am, I know this is hard. I've been doing this for decades and no matter what, it's not easy. Maybe it's easier for you to see the man first. He has a tattoo. Do you want to confirm that before you're asked to look?"

Caroline hated the tattoo and here she was now using it to identify her husband. "It's of a cartoon bird. It's yellow," she said flatly. Officer Kelly looked at Dr. Isaac, who nodded.

"Yes, this man does have that. The woman has a lot of tattoos, too," he said. "Can you remember any of those?"

"Yes," replied Caroline. "She has several of random things. But one says 'Loyola.'"

Dr. Isaac nodded. "Those both match up, I'm sorry to say," he said and paused. "Should we have a look at the man?"

Caroline nodded. This all felt so standard, like going to the doctor. Meanwhile, she noticed Officer Kelly seemed relieved that Dr. Isaac was there to help.

"Okay, let's take a look then," he said and walked over to one vault.

Opening it carefully, he pulled out a stretcher with a body bag. Looking over at Caroline, he motioned for her to come over.

"Are you ready?" he asked.

She stood up and began to walk toward him. Officer Kelly noticed how she began to shake so he stood next to her, linking his arm through hers.

"Thank you," she said hoarsely.

As she got to the bagged body, Dr. Isaac unzipped the top part showing the head. Caroline gasped and put her hands to her mouth. Tears began to stream down her swollen cheeks.

"Yes, that's him," she choked out and nuzzled her head into Officer Kelly's shoulder and took a few steps back.

"Okay, then," said Dr. Isaac. "One more and then we're done."

He zipped the bag up and rolled the body bag into the vault. Moving to the next one, he opened it, pulled the stretcher out, and unzipped.

"Come take a quick look," he said.

Officer Kelly guided her over.

"Can you please look really quick like Dr. Isaac asked?" he said.

Caroline nodded, pulling her head away from the comfort of his shoulder and took a few steps forward again.

Looking down, she knew that face. She nodded to the two men to indicate that it was her friend.

"Yes, that's her," she finally said.

But instead of pulling away from the body, she pulled away from Officer Kelly and moved closer to the woman on the table. She reached her hand out to stroke Noel's cold cheek.

"Yes, this is my friend. Her name is Noel," she choked out.

She rubbed her fingers up and down Noel's right cheek.

"She's so cold," she said.

Dr. Isaac nodded.

"May I have a moment?" asked Caroline.

Dr. Isaac nodded and headed toward the door with Officer Kelly behind him. As they reached the hallway, the two men noticed two young women walking down the hall.

"Those are her daughters," said Officer Kelly.

"Understood," said Dr. Isaac. "Funny how she reacted. I haven't seen a wife hide from the husband yet go to the friend like that before. Strange."

Meanwhile, as Caroline stood over Noel, she began to cry harder.

"How did this happen to you?" she asked, now stroking her friend's hair. "How did this happen to you?"

There was a knock at the door, and she turned to see the girls standing there with tears running down their cheeks. She nodded her head and they began to cry more, turning to embrace one another.

Caroline turned from Noel and walked to the door. The girls reached out their arms to embrace her. As the three hugged, Dr. Isaac and Officer Kelly exchanged looks, unsure of what to do.

Caroline pulled out of the hug and wiped her eyes. She looked at the two men and said, "Now what do we do? How do we find out what happened?"

CHAPTER 37

MOUNT KATAHDIN, MAINE

Tuesday, May 11, at 5:47 a.m.

Waking up on Tuesday, Marigold knew she had to go into work but dreaded it. The knot in her stomach was tight. Her head throbbed from the whiskey the night before. But it was almost 6:00 a.m., and she had to get the twins off to school and get herself ready for work.

Two hours later, she was in the car, childless, on her way to work. Pulling into the driveway, she noticed a few other cars in front. She drove to the back of the inn and parked next to Marcus's truck.

She entered through the back door into the kitchen, the warm aroma of coffee and freshly cooked eggs filling her nose. Instead of wanting to eat, she wanted to vomit. She had covered the left side of her face when she drove by the pond and dam, trying to avoid the images of the trash bag filling her head.

Marcus turned when he heard her come in. His face was drawn and he looked surprised to see her.

"Why are you here?" he asked. "Maybe you shouldn't be here."

"Why do you say that?" snapped Marigold. "A woman needs to work regardless of the shit she sees every day up in this dump."

Marcus dropped his spatula, letting the eggs burn. He hurried to her and grabbed her by the shoulders.

"Maybe you shouldn't be here, I said," he snapped at her. Marigold felt nervous but didn't want him to know. She had to be strong.

"And why is that? What? Am I gonna get fired? Good. Let 'em," she said and tried to wiggle from his tight grip.

"Listen, girl," he said. "They checked in last night."

"Who checked in?" Marigold snapped back.

Then she realized who he meant. "Oh," she said and stepped back as he released her.

"They called me in last night to be here, the owners did," said Marcus. "I came in late and had to get a room ready for them and a meal. I had some fiddlehead soup and bread around so I made that with some fried ham."

"Marcus, I don't care what you fed them," said Marigold. "Jesus, what did they say? What do they look like?"

She headed to the counter, taking a seat at one of the bar stools. Marcus poured her a cup of coffee, sliding it across the counter to her waiting hand.

"They look like normal people," he said. "One middle-aged woman and two youngish girls like in their twenties. They look kind of preppy. Officer Kelly called yesterday that he needed a few rooms for them and for some doctor who had helped out. I guess they came up last night to look at the bodies, and it seems like the two are their family."

"They are?" gasped Marigold. "What else did they say? Did they talk to you?"

"Nah, not really," he replied. "This morning one of the girls came down. She seemed kind of bitchy. She got a couple of coffees and went back upstairs. I didn't tell her nothing. I don't think they know that the bodies were found across the street and all."

Marigold took a big gulp of coffee. For a moment, she forgot about her hangover. As she did, a woman walked through the door. She was attractive but sheepish.

"Good morning," the woman greeted them.

"Good morning," replied Marcus and Marigold.

As the woman walked to look at the food placed out on the table, Marcus raised his eyebrows indicating to Marigold that this was the woman.

"What's good today?" she asked.

"Oh, it's all good," replied Marigold, getting up from the bar.

She was curious as to who this woman was. Moving to stand next to her, she smiled awkwardly and tried to grab the woman's eye.

"Marcus makes the best eggs," said Marigold and pointed to the plate. "What's your name, ma'am?"

The woman glanced at her quickly and reached for a plate.

"My name is Caroline," she said.

Marigold couldn't help herself. "Are you related to the people that we found?" she blurted out.

Caroline looked up startled. It hadn't occurred to her that someone had found them, that a real person had stumbled across their bodies. Marcus dropped his head, frustrated with Marigold's blunt approach.

"Uh, yes, I am," Caroline replied. "I believe it's my best friend, Noel, and my husband, Greg."

"I, uh, shouldn't have said that," Marigold said, realizing how it must have sounded.

"Did you find them?" Caroline asked.

"Yeah, I found her," replied Marigold.

"I don't know much," Caroline said. "But I know it's them. I saw the bodies last night. Officer Kelly suggested that we stay here along with Dr. Isaac, who's helping him out. How did you find them?"

"Can you take a walk?" asked Marigold.

She wanted a smoke and wanted to share what she knew. If this had been happening to her, she felt she'd want to know everything. Caroline nodded, putting the plate of food down and following Marigold out the door. Marcus waved, not wanting to be involved.

"Have you come up here before?" asked Marigold as they walked along the dusty driveway.

She led the way but quickly the woman got next to her, crossing her arms in front of her as Marigold pulled her cigarettes out of her pocket and lit one.

"No," said Caroline. "I never even knew this place existed. One of my daughters came up to Maine for college, but that's the extent. I have twin girls who are twenty-seven."

"It's called down Maine," said Marigold. "Never understood why but down Maine. Not up Maine."

"Oh," replied Caroline. "Down Maine."

The two walked down the driveway, past the front of the inn toward the lake and the dam.

"Will you tell me what you know?" asked Caroline. "You found them both?"

Marigold took a deep puff.

"I found one," she began. "A tourist found the other one down the street. Well, half."

"Half?" Caroline asked confused.

Marigold gulped, almost choking on the smoke in her lungs. "I assumed you knew."

"I don't know much," replied Caroline. "This has all been such a whirlwind. Tell me what happened."

As the two walked, Marigold told Caroline about the bag and how it was nagging at her until she went over and found the body. The two began to cross the street. Caroline noticed the police tape.

"So, this is it?" Caroline asked, examining the tape, the grass, the dam, and the lake.

Marigold nodded, pulling another cigarette from the pack in her pocket.

"Yeah, this is where I found the first part of her," Marigold said.

"I'm sorry. What?" said Caroline. "You keep saying 'half' and I don't know what you mean."

"I don't know how else to say it, so here it is," said Marigold and stopped to face Caroline. "I found half of her here. In a trash bag. A tourist found your man and the bottom half of her down the street."

Caroline's face turned white. Never had she imagined anything like this. Dr. Isaac only showed her the faces of each and nothing more.

"Want a cigarette?" asked Marigold.

To Caroline's own surprise, she nodded. Marigold took the lit cigarette out of her mouth and handed it to Caroline, who took a drag followed by a long cough.

"Half of her was here? And half was down the street?" Caroline repeated once she caught her breath.

"Yeah," replied Marigold.

Caroline began walking around the outside of the police tape.

"Can we walk down there?" she asked.

She couldn't cry. She couldn't process. She just had to see where they had found Greg.

"We sure can," said Marigold, and the two ventured down the street.

Trying to fill the silence, Marigold told her about her own twin grandchildren, her life in Maine, and her job at the inn. Caroline nodded, still trying to be polite while also trying to avoid her own reality.

On the horizon, Caroline could see the tape. As they got closer, Caroline ventured up the embankment. She threw the dwindling cigarette into the grass and then stepped on it to smother it. The taste reminded her of the time she tried one of Noel's cigarettes in college and threw it out. But years later, after graduation, they would sometimes have one or two with Greg on the stoop in Beacon Hill as he smoked a cigar.

"This is where they found the guy," said Marigold. "I mean, your husband. And the rest of your friend."

Caroline began again to walk around the police tape, eyeing over the shrubs. She bent down to touch the grass. Maybe if she looked hard enough, she'd find a clue or something to help her understand how this happened.

"Do you know anything more?" Caroline asked, standing up and looking back to Marigold.

"I don't know nothing more," said Marigold.

Out of the corner of her eye, Caroline saw the girls walking down the street.

"These are my girls," said Caroline. "Please don't tell them about the body of Noel being in two."

"Noel?" asked Marigold. Then she realized it. The woman's name was Noel.

"What a pretty name," she said. "What about the man?"

"His name is Greg," answered Caroline. "Or, I guess, was Greg."

The girls got closer, eyeing Marigold up and down.

"Girls, this is...oh gosh, what's your name?" said Caroline.

"Marigold," she said and reached out a hand.

"I'm Amanda," said Amanda, shaking her head.

Jackie just waved. "Jackie," she said quickly.

"Do either of you girls want a cigarette?" offered Marigold, unsure of what to say. Both shook their heads no.

"Marigold found Noel and another gentleman found your father here," Caroline explained.

The girls began walking around the area like their mother, unsure of what to do.

"I should go," said Marigold, leaving the three to investigate.

Heading back to the inn, she told Marcus what happened. She noticed the doctor was having breakfast. She started on her chores, moving from room to room, and eventually got to the master suite, where she noticed laundry baskets tucked in corners of the room. Examining the belongings, she realized it was theirs. On the nightstand was a photo of all five people—the twin girls, Caroline, Greg, Noel, and a dog. It looked recent, perhaps taken at Christmas.

Marigold picked it up and sat on the bed squinting at the faces of the two dead people. They were alive, happy, and laughing. How did these people end up here cold and dead? A tear came to her eye. She looked up and out the window, noticing the three women across the street examining where she had first found the body.

CHAPTER 38

MOUNT KATAHDIN, MAINE

Tuesday, May 11, at 9:18 a.m.

O fficer Kelly had a list of questions ready to ask the family. He and Dr. Isaac had discussed what to ask in the morning as they watched the women walk the scene. Officer Kelly had arrived at the inn right after Caroline had left with Marigold. They spoke in hushed voices when the girls came down the stairs asking Marcus in the kitchen where their mother was.

While Officer Kelly was ready to interview each person individually and the family together, he wanted to make sure he was asking the right questions. Over coffee and blueberry muffins, Dr. Isaac gave him ideas on questions to ask. He typed furiously on his phone trying to get every word down and committed to memory.

"Try to get each of them to get comfortable, you know, and trust you, son. One of them may know something, whether this was intentional or not. You need to get to those clues," explained Dr. Isaac. "Take it slow. Listen to your gut. Make sure you record everything both on your tape recorder and the video in the room. Once you get all that, you can review it on your own and with the team down in Portland who can assist in analyzing the body language and tone."

Officer Kelly nodded and typed. He was ready to do this. He was ready to solve the case and knew that he could do it.

When Officer Kelly was done talking to Dr. Isaac, he walked across the street. The three women looked at him and then back down as they walked back and forth around the police-taped area.

"Good morning," he began. "I was hoping you'd all come down to the station later on today so I can ask you all some questions to try to figure this all out."

Caroline nodded in agreement. "What time do you need us?" she asked. "What are the clues telling you now about this?"

Officer Kelly wanted to be confident but honest. He, like Dr. Isaac said, needed to build trust.

"I don't have much, which is why I need your help," he said. "Maybe just after lunch?"

"What do you mean you don't have much?" snapped Jackie. "What else do you have going on up here to figure out? Finding a moose to arrest?"

Caroline turned her head giving her daughter a sharp look. "We'll be there at 12:30," she replied.

At 12:15 p.m., the three women went down to the station. Officer Kelly met them at the door and asked them to take a seat in the conference room. He had downloaded an app to record the interviews and set up video cameras in various corners of the room. He was determined not to miss anything and had another officer in the room with him to take notes.

Sitting at one side of the table facing the three women on the other side, he began with his list of questions.

"Did anyone want to harm any of you or your husband and friend that you know of?" he started with.

Caroline told him no.

"Did either have any sort of issues going on with others? Maybe at work or bad business deals?" he asked.

Caroline told him no.

"Do you know of any affairs that either had together or with others that may have caused this to happen?" he asked.

Caroline again told him no.

Officer Kelly started to get nervous. He asked more questions. Caroline answered most, stating that she didn't know of any issues or problems or reasons why this could have happened. The girls responded a few times, but Caroline led in answering. She did tell him about Greg's few surprise weekends away and how it surprised her but seemed all business.

"Maybe it's time to talk to you each individually," he finally said, feeling tired and frustrated by the lack of movement in getting answers.

He also wondered if the girls knew something that the mother didn't, or if Caroline was hiding something.

"I can go first," said Jackie. "Do I need a lawyer?"

Caroline rolled her eyes. She was angry and frustrated, too. Feeling dumbfounded with what had gone on, she didn't know what else to say to Officer Kelly and the lenses staring at her from around the room. She, like her husband and friend, was a victim to this and she was feeling like a criminal when all she wanted was answers herself.

"No, I don't foresee you needing a lawyer at this point," said Officer Kelly. "We can start with you."

Caroline and Amanda stood up and walked out of the room. Similar to the first round, Officer Kelly asked Jackie question after question. She didn't seem to know anything more than her mother. After an hour, he asked her to get her sister. Maybe Amanda would know more.

Amanda came into the room. She seemed shy and had a deeper sadness to her than her mother and sister. Officer Kelly started again with the same set of questions. Amanda told him about her strained relationship with her dad and her complete fondness and travels with Noel.

She told him about their trips to Spain and Italy, and how Noel was like a second mother to her, always encouraging her to follow her dreams.

"Tell me more about Noel," he asked, wanting to leave it open to see what other information he could gather.

"My mother doesn't know this," began Amanda and started squirming in her chair. "But Noel had a new tattoo that she didn't want my mom to know about. I don't really know why. Noel had a ton of tattoos and my mom knew about most of them, I think, except this one, which seemed weird."

"What was the tattoo?" asked Officer Kelly, getting excited that he may have gotten a new lead.

"It was of a butterfly," she said.

"What does that signify?" he asked.

Amanda shrugged. "I think it was a college thing and maybe had something to do with my dad."

"Why do you say that?" inquired Officer Kelly.

"My dad in college was really into Jeeps and my mom made him get rid of his when they moved to Boston after college. I guess he was always kind of upset about that," Amanda explained. "But he and Noel used to go out riding in his and she told me those were some of the happiest times in her life riding around in that Jeep with him out in western Massachusetts. Sometimes they'd stop and she'd catch butterflies. I promised her I'd never tell my mom about it. She only got it a few weeks ago. It was wicked new."

"Do you think they were having an affair or something?" asked Officer Kelly, feeling like he had finally cracked more into the case and was getting somewhere.

Amanda shrugged, which surprised Officer Kelly.

"I don't know," she began. "One time when I was a kid, I saw them in the hall together and it always stuck with me. His arm was resting on her back. I mean, maybe it wasn't a big deal. But it felt strange and I remember that feeling. I was always so close to my dad before that, but after...I just felt like I couldn't trust him. I don't know why that was and I was too young to really realize what may have been happening, but I just knew at the time it wasn't right. I never told anyone or brought it up to either one of them."

Officer Kelly thought back to Dr. Isaac's comments about trusting his gut.

"When your mother talked about your dad going off for weekends, do you think that was connected?" asked Officer Kelly.

Amanda thought for a moment.

"No, I don't think so. I think that's just kind of random," answered Amanda. "Noel travels all the time and that's just part of who she is. My dad, since we moved out, tried to refocus on his career since we were not around. I guess, yeah, in some ways it may be odd to do something like this but he's outgoing and driven."

"What about your mom?" he asked.

"She works for the local paper and has been trying to make more friends, but she kind of keeps to herself, unlike those two. They were kind of like peas in a pod or whatever the saying is. They were still close and talked and my mom had them and a few other friends, but that was always kind of it," said Amanda.

"Did your dad or Noel ever come up here before? Your mother mentioned you went to college in Maine." asked Officer Kelly.

"I think he did, yes," Amanda said. "One time, he played hooky from work to get lunch with me at school maybe like in my junior year. I was surprised. He had never done that before. After lunch he said he was headed farther north, which surprised me since it was late in the day for him to not be headed home and to simply be skipping work. I don't know what he did, but he left and then Mom said he hadn't come home that night. I didn't want to rat on him for skipping work and seeing me and trying, so I never told her that either. It was weird, too, since my mom said she couldn't reach Noel around that time, too."

Officer Kelly took notes as fast as he could, filling up his notebook with Amanda's stories of her father and Noel. The other officer in the room was writing furiously, too. In the margins, Officer Kelly jotted down her body movements, tone, and other questions he had. Like why did Noel and Greg both seem to trust Amanda with things like skipping work and tattoos that neither Jackie nor Caroline knew about?

Officer Kelly wondered about secret lives, affairs, or owed money—the stuff you see in the movies. He also wondered about his next steps, once he analyzed all the information and notes he had gathered. Amanda said she was tired and it was almost 5:00 p.m. Officer Kelly was tired, too, and he was anxious to tell Dr. Isaac what he had found out.

After thanking Amanda and then Jackie and Caroline, he told them they could head back to the inn for the night and that he wanted to see them again the next day. They agreed. Once they were out of sight, he smiled to himself. He was doing it. He was solving a crime.

CHAPTER 39

MOUNT KATAHDIN, MAINE

Tuesday, May 11, at 7:11 p.m.

Later Tuesday night, Caroline sat in the living room of the inn, a glass of wine in hand, facing out to where Noel had been found. Taking a sip, she thought about her friendship with Noel and how she'd fill this void in her life. She didn't want to admit it, but she wondered who she'd miss more, Greg or Noel. The thought made her shudder.

Caroline pulled out her phone. News of them identifying the bodies hadn't quite spread yet, but she assumed people had begun to figure it out based on the family's posts. It was just a matter of time until she would have to speak about it openly. Caroline dreaded it.

Scrolling through social media, she noticed a friend request. Thinking it was odd with the timing of all that was going on, she clicked to see who the request was from and her jaw dropped. It was Matt Cooper. Her Matt. Her Matt from her college years, whom she had thought was "the one."

Over the years, she had checked his profile but was fearful of sending the request herself. What if Greg found out or saw it? What if Matt ignored it? While her cursor had hovered over the "Add Friend" button over the years, she never had the courage to click. She stalked quietly under the cover of night and under the excuse of too much wine.

But here he was in her life again through the innocence of a friend request. There was no Greg to worry about now, and there was no Noel to tell how ironic this was. But it felt dirty. It felt weird. Caroline put her phone down, her heart racing. It was wrong to feel this excited while she was dealing with her husband and her friend being murdered. And now here was Matt.

She took another sip of wine and feared that having too much may inhibit the request from Officer Kelly to reflect on who would have done this. She had so much to think about, but now Matt was on the forefront of her thoughts.

"Mom?"

Caroline turned. It was Jackie. "Hi honey, come sit," Caroline said. She was thankful for her daughter's interruption to her own thoughts.

"Mom, what do you think happened to Dad and Noel?" Jackie asked. "The cop guy kept asking me all sorts of questions. Questions that I couldn't even answer. Do you really think something was going on between Dad and Noel that would have led to this? Or that Dad had something weird going on?"

Caroline had thought about it. Over the years, she wondered if more had gone on with Greg and Noel in college or even since. But when those thoughts came into her mind, she pushed them out. It wouldn't have made sense. The two could have easily been together in college, so why hide it?

Even after college, she and Greg could have easily broken up if Noel and Greg had wanted to be together. But any time she asked either one during their alone time, they both denied anything more ever happening or wanting to be with each other.

Over time, she began to trust that. Although she did, this did bring new concerns to her mind that maybe they had been lying through the years. The thought hurt, but it wasn't as bad as knowing both were dead now. Yet, what if it could have been avoided? If the two were into something more and that led to this somehow?

Caroline knew Jackie needed comfort. Although Jackie acted tough, Caroline knew she was struggling as much as Amanda. The only difference was that Amanda showed her pain.

"Jackie," she began, placing her hand on Jackie's. "I know this is hard. This is something none of us could have expected. I don't think anything was going on with your father and Noel."

"But, Mom, how do you know? What if Dad had, like, a bad business deal, like these people are saying, and that made this happen?" asked Jackie.

"Jackie, maybe this is something to do with your dad. I don't know. Or maybe it was Noel. I don't know. Maybe this was just some huge, terrible misunderstanding. I don't know," said Caroline.

She, like her daughter, was concerned and didn't have the answers. "Want some wine?" she offered.

Jackie shook her head and left the room.

Caroline's mind filled with thoughts again about how this happened and why someone would have been so brutal in their murders. She knew about Noel's body from Marigold, and Officer Kelly had quickly mentioned the bullet in Greg's head at one point, but it just seemed cruel and unusual for two very normal people to both be murdered—and murdered in this way.

Picking up her phone, she reopened her social media profile. Matt's friend request was still there. She accepted it.

CHAPTER 40

MOUNT KATAHDIN, MAINE

Wednesday, May 12, at 7:48 a.m.

The next day, Marigold came to work and found Caroline and the girls in the kitchen. They looked tired, and Marcus was cooking them eggs again. Caroline had been up all night thinking about what she was going to do next, but also about Matt and his request to connect. Now he'd be in her feed and there'd be no more secret looking. He would just be there.

"What's up for the day?" asked Marcus, trying to break the silence.

"Back down to the police station," replied Amanda. She was feeling guilty about what she had said but knew it was the right thing to do telling Officer Kelly. She was being honest about what she knew. Maybe it would help, but maybe it was nothing. Now she had to think about telling her mother and sister.

"That Officer Kelly is a good guy," said Marigold. "He means well. He's good folk."

Caroline nodded and smiled, trying not to be rude. "We're going to head down there in a few to get a jump on this. I need to talk to him more about funerals and how we work that along with everything else," said Caroline.

"Getting right down to business, huh, Mom?" said Jackie.

Amanda kicked her sister under the table.

"Ouch!" cried Jackie.

"Let's get going," said Caroline, wanting to change the scenery and conversation.

The ride was quiet down to the station. Amanda drove. When they got there, Officer Kelly came to the door, ushering them into the conference room. He had been up most of the night reviewing his notes and the video and audio recordings. Dr. Isaac had headed home but had called Officer Kelly to hear his thoughts.

Officer Kelly told him about the comments from Amanda and how Jackie and Caroline didn't seem to know anything. Dr. Isaac summed it up to one of two things. Maybe they truly didn't know and something was going on that Amanda may have realized or noticed throughout the years. Or maybe Jackie and Caroline were lying and trying to cover up a plan to murder the two due to an ongoing affair.

Dr. Isaac encouraged Officer Kelly to share what Amanda told him with the other two women. Maybe this would spur their memories or push them to finally speak more openly about what they knew.

"Should I be concerned about this?" asked Officer Kelly. "Should she be the one to tell them, not me?"

"Son, of course you should," replied Dr. Isaac. "You're in over your head and investigating a double homicide. You have three people who may know the answers in your back pocket and you're acting like a doofus about it."

The words rang in Officer Kelly's mind. He wanted to do the right thing. He wanted to do a good job.

Welcoming the women back, he decided to take a different approach. He was going to be tough. Maine tough. He was going to get to the bottom of this. As the women sat, he picked up his notebook, flipping through its pages.

"You know, ladies," he began, "something isn't right here. Not right at all."

He slammed the notebook on the table. All three jumped. He hoped this act of aggression would scare them to talk.

"Amanda, you had a lot to say yesterday. A lot. Maybe you should share with your mother and sister," he said and crossed his arms.

Amanda began to cry.

"Amanda, what do you know?" asked Caroline, visibly concerned and surprised that either of the girls knew anything suspicious.

"Jesus, Amanda, stop crying! What do you know?" demanded Jackie.

Amanda's tears began to flow more and she put her head in her hands. The guilt of knowing these things was killing her and she was scared to tell her mother and sister about the incident from years ago and the latest tattoo.

Officer Kelly felt terrible about making the young woman cry. But he was determined to get to the bottom of this today. He needed answers based on demands from his supervisor, and he wanted approval from Dr. Isaac. He was also concerned about the increase in media attention overnight as word had spread of the victims' identities. It was beginning to flood the local and national news.

"Amanda, tell me," said Caroline, putting her hand on Amanda's shoulder. "It's okay. We just need to know to help figure out what happened to Daddy and Noel."

Amanda lifted her head and began to tell the story, from when she saw them together as a child in the hall to Noel's recent butterfly tattoo. Jackie's face turned white and then filled with rage, while Caroline's eyes widened in confusion.

"Amanda, you are so fucking dumb," said Jackie, standing up. "You think that any of that shit has to do with them being murdered in east bumfuck Maine? Dumb. Dumb. Dumb," she spat and walked out of the room.

Officer Kelly looked at her in shock but let her go. He was more interested in how Caroline would react. This would be telling.

"Are you sure you saw him do that?" she asked, surprised by the statement and how her youngest twin had kept this secret for so long.

Caroline did believe Greg and Noel, although she sometimes had her doubts. But maybe more was going on, even in her own house.

"Yes, Mom," Amanda cried, looking up. She heaved and tried to catch her breath. "I wanted to tell you, but I was scared."

Caroline rubbed Amanda's shoulder. She thought back to when Amanda was younger, and how she and Greg had always had a great relationship. And then one day it just stopped. She had always wondered why and attributed it to growing up and the father-daughter dynamic changing. It never occurred to her that maybe she witnessed something that changed her.

The tattoo was surprising. Caroline knew that Greg loved that Jeep and was mad that he had to sell it but didn't think it was that big of a deal. She knew that Noel and Greg would sometimes go off riding in it during college, but she didn't realize that Noel appreciated that time so much as to get the memory of it engraved on her body with a butterfly. Caroline knew she had to support her daughter and take her own concerns out of the picture.

"Ma'am, you didn't know any of this?" inquired Officer Kelly, trying to get Caroline to break and tell more of what she potentially knew.

"No," she told him and continued to rub Amanda's back.

"What else do you know then?" he demanded.

Caroline began to get angry.

"I told you I don't know much," she began. "This is news to me, too. What are you hiding?" she inquired. "I heard from that woman at the inn about how my friend was chopped in half. And you mentioned quickly about the hole in my husband's head. What else do you know? Are you even talking to Massachusetts police who may be able to actually help, instead of this shit?"

Amanda looked at her, stunned. "Cut in half?" she croaked.

Caroline was too angry at this point. "Yes, dear, cut in half," she said. Looking back at Officer Kelly, she said, "What else do you know?"

He was stunned and nervous.

"She was choked to death and then cut in half," he said blankly. Both of their faces dropped.

"Choked?" asked Caroline. "She was fucking choked and you are just telling me that now?"

He nodded.

"Give me a fucking break," Caroline said. "Get someone on this case who knows what the fuck they are doing and then contact us. We're leaving and getting a lawyer. Get up, Amanda," she instructed.

Amanda did and the two walked out of the room.

Jackie stood at the door on her phone. "What happened?" she asked.

"We're going back home, that's what happened," snapped Caroline. "I'm done with this shit."

Getting into the car, the trio ventured back to the inn to pack. As Jackie drove, Caroline pulled out her phone and began texting friends for suggestions on lawyers who may be able to help.

Her mind raced with what to do next. Out of habit, she navigated to social media to post something there. When she logged in, there were messages waiting for her with condolences as the news spread of who the unidentified bodies were. She scrolled through, glancing at each. And then she saw it. It was from Matt simply saying: "Hi. How are you? I heard about Greg."

CHAPTER 41

SOMEWHERE IN VERMONT

Caroline and Matt, thirty-three years ago

When Caroline thought about Matt over the years, her mind would dance over the times he'd lay his head on her shoulder and she'd play with his curly dark brown hair. She'd think about how he had smelled like fresh cut grass and wore ripped jeans and flannels and how he sometimes smelled like pot or cloves from smoking.

Yet, her favorite memory was from the time the two left campus and took a weekend trip to Vermont in early May. On the way up, they stopped and had a picnic at a lake. Matt laid down a blanket from the back of his Jeep and the two drank Vermont beer over sandwiches.

He had put his head in her lap and had kissed her thighs where her jean shorts were frayed. It made her giggle.

"What are you thinking about?" he had asked, which was unlike him. Normally, Matt was kind of quiet, aloof, the strong silent type with his curly hair, long frame, and sparkling green eyes. Caroline was surprised by the question.

She looked at him and then up at the clouds, trying to find the best answer. She was so nervous around him and felt like she couldn't completely be herself. But she liked the way it felt because the nervousness made her feel alive and young. She spun a finger through one of his curls as she thought.

"I don't know," she finally responded, not wanting to keep him waiting. She couldn't be honest that she was thinking about him and a life with him outside of school.

"Come on, you have to be thinking about something," demanded Matt, sitting up and putting his nose to hers.

"What are you thinking about?" he whispered. Caroline laughed, pulling back.

"What are you thinking?" he asked again, putting his face to hers again and began making a chomping sound with his mouth. "I'm going to eat your face if you don't tell me."

Caroline laughed and lay back on the blanket. Matt straddled her and put his mouth to her ear, still chomping.

"Mmmm, tastes so good," he said. His breath smelled like hops from the beer.

"Fine, fine," yelped Caroline. "I'm thinking about you. I'm always thinking about you."

He laughed. "You are not," he cried. "You think about school since you're a huge dork. Dork, dork, dork."

"I am not," she spat back, hitting his chest.

He kissed her. Then he lay next to her, putting his head on her shoulder. The two breathed heavily. Caroline felt happy. But she wondered why he didn't believe her.

"I do think about you all the time," she said.

He looked up at her and smiled. "I know you do, my girl. My Carli. I know you do," he said.

The two lay there staring up at the clouds dancing across the sky. Caroline began to doze from the beer. She felt Matt dozing, too. They stayed there for hours, falling in and out of sleep with their arms wrapped around each other, although it was hot for Vermont that day and sweat was dripping down Caroline's back.

While a part of her wanted to get up and move to a cooler spot, another part wanted to stay right there in the moment with him forever. She tried to let herself give in to the feeling. It was like nothing she had ever felt before.

Matt made her feel seen. He made her feel wanted. He also made her feel a little uncomfortable because of how vulnerable she wanted to be with him. After some time, Matt lifted his sleepy head, his curls everywhere. He placed his face against hers. She could still smell the beer on his breath.

"I love you, Caroline," he said and smiled. Then he leaned in to kiss her lips gently.

"I love you, too," she said, kissing him back.

He rested his head back down and she again twisted her fingers through his curls. She wanted him forever.

CHAPTER 42

MOUNT KATAHDIN, MAINE

Wednesday, May 12, at 12:01 p.m.

Officer Kelly was annoyed that the family had left but understood their frustrations and hurt. There was nothing he could offer them in terms of answers, and his gut told him they weren't involved with the murders.

He texted Marigold after the trio had left his office. She told him they were at the inn packing up.

* * * * *

Caroline moved slowly, unsure of what to do herself. She couldn't tell anyone about Matt messaging her. And she knew that her thoughts moving from the circumstances to him would sound insane. What would people say?

"Your husband and friend have been viciously murdered and all you can think about is an ex-boyfriend from college?" she heard over and over again in her head.

As the girls packed, she explained to Marigold that she didn't think it was smart of them to be there anymore. They were going to head home and would get help there. Marigold listened, nodding as Caroline spoke. She told her she wasn't sure what else they could do, if anything.

"Want my number?" Marigold asked. "In case you wanna text or anything?"

Caroline nodded. She thought it may not be a bad idea in case anything else came up or she thought of questions that maybe Marigold could help with.

"Can I talk to you, you know, like alone for a minute?" asked Marigold.

Caroline was surprised by the request but nodded and the two headed into the hallway. Pulling a key from her pocket, Marigold unlocked the room next door and the two women walked in.

* * * * *

Marigold wasn't quite sure what she was going to say but felt like she had to connect somehow with Caroline before she left.

"Ma'am," she began, feeling somewhat unsure of how to begin. "I mean, Caroline," she corrected. "I can't say that I know how you feel or ever will. God only knows that I've seen some shit in my own life, but this is like nothing I've seen before."

Caroline nodded.

"But I just want you to know that if you ever need me, you can call or text. You know, I don't know how I can help but feel like I should say that, seeing how I found your friend," she explained.

She wanted to tell Caroline about how she felt connected to her and her girls based on this but wasn't sure how she could say that without it sounding strange.

"Thank you, Marigold," said Caroline reaching her hands to hers. "I know you want to help, and I appreciate you and that."

Marigold nodded. There was nothing else she could say. Caroline left the room and Marigold went back to her phone. Officer Kelly had texted her again asking her to let him know when they left because he was going to come down.

A few moments later, the family was in the car. Marigold texted Officer Kelly letting him know they were leaving. She and Marcus had given them final hugs and said again how sorry they were. The white SUV sped out of the driveway and past where Noel had been found.

* * * * *

Officer Kelly headed toward the inn, passing the family on his way. He pulled up and saw Marcus and Marigold standing outside.

Getting out of the car, he looked at one and then the other.

"Do you think they had anything to do with this? Did they say anything suspicious or do anything you'd consider to be strange while they were here?" Officer Kelly asked.

Marcus laughed and looked annoyed. "Nah, sir, get out of here. They are just a sad family," he said and walked back into the inn.

"What do you think?" he asked Marigold. "Think they have anything to do with it?"

Marigold pulled her cigarettes out of her pocket and lit one as her gaze moved to where she had first seen the trash bag.

"No, they didn't have anything to do with this," she said. "Something happened to these people. Something really bad, like we know. But those ladies seem like good people. They don't have anything to do with this."

Officer Kelly nodded. He had talked to Dr. Isaac and others on the case. He had spoken to other local troublemakers who were tree cutters and all had denied being involved. But something wasn't right in how these two people from Massachusetts got all the way up to Maine and ended up like this.

"I gotta get back to work," said Marigold, turning to head back inside. Officer Kelly nodded and headed across the street to walk both scenes again. He was convinced he'd missed a clue and was determined to find something that would help him solve the case.

Dipping under the crime scene tape, he looked carefully at each blade of grass. They were all so clean. There were a few spots of dark brown spattered across some of the blades from when the body had been removed. After some time, he walked further along the street and examined scene two. Still nothing. Still clean.

CHAPTER 43

NEWBURYPORT, MASSACHUSETTS

Wednesday, June 9,
at 5:32 p.m.

Four weeks later, Caroline was sitting on the porch having a glass of wine, Rose at her feet. She had talked to a few lawyers in Boston over the previous weeks. Both girls had stayed with her for two weeks before they decided it was time to get somewhat back to normal. Normal for all three of them now was crying on and off throughout the day and before bed.

The services for Greg and Noel had been held on two separate days, one right after the other, to help with those traveling into town. It had rained terribly on both days, yet hundreds of people showed up. Even Officer Kelly and Marigold had made the trip together—Marigold to show respect and Officer Kelly to investigate.

Caroline herself was apprehensive to have Matt come. The whole thing surprised her. When she had arrived home from Maine, she toyed with replying to Matt. Would that look tacky and inappropriate? But after a few glasses of wine and wanting to feel connected to someone, she pulled out her phone and replied back saying hello and letting him know that something terrible had happened.

To her surprise and delight, Matt began to type back right away, telling her that he learned about what was going on from social media.

Matt: Is it true what they are saying? Both Greg and Noel were murdered and left up in Maine? Obvi you and Noel were so close for years and you got with Greg in college, too. Wow, I don't even know what to say.

Caroline took a sip of wine and began to type back. She felt angry by his response and how he said she "got with Greg." She started dating Greg because she felt so mad at Matt and wanted to find someone else. And she was never strong enough or motivated enough to end it with him and maybe she should have.

She knew it was the wine making her mad. She had had a good life with Greg, regardless of what was going on now. It had been comfortable and happy, normal and regular. While she missed both, she wished that Noel was here to talk with her about Matt's sudden reappearance.

Caroline: Yes, I'm afraid so…I can't believe this happened.

The conversation changed from talk of the situation to talk of the past and what each had done since college. Caroline found herself chatting with Matt long past midnight.

When she told him about the arrangements and her plans for their services and funerals, she was shocked when he offered to fly in.

Matt: I could come. I knew them, too, and would be honored to support you and your family. I don't want to make it weird. I know we kind of dated in college.

This response made her mad, too. *Kind of dated*, she thought, like it hadn't been years on and off of him being so quiet and laid back sometimes mixed with moments of silliness that made her feel happy yet uncomfortable, followed by months of being ghosted and ignored for no reason. Then when he eventually left school to move to California, it made her feel unloved and unseen, hence forcing her to go out with Greg to fill the void.

Caroline stopped responding when he said that. She needed some space. But the next morning she woke up to a text from him with a screenshot of a booked flight to Boston. She felt happy and sad all at the same time.

When Matt first pulled up to the house, she watched from a top floor window, holding one of the drapes in front of her for cover. She felt like a child. Even Rose stood from afar giving her a strange look. When Matt got out of the car, her heart fluttered. His hair was still curly and mostly dark brown with some white. He looked thin and toned. He was wearing jeans, a shirt with a blazer over it, and loafers.

It was a far cry from the flannels and ripped jeans of the past, but he still had that swagger of not giving a fuck. She smiled and let go of the drape, heading down the stairs to greet him at the door.

She opened the door and he smiled warmly at her, his blazer now in hand. "My Carli," he said and leaned in to kiss her cheek.

"It's so great to see you," she said and placed her hand on his chest as he pulled away.

He smelled different. Not of grass and weed anymore but rich cologne and leather.

"You look amazing," he said, looking her up and down.

She was wearing a white dress with flowers. Although she had been drinking wine every night to deal with her feelings and to feel confident enough to talk to him, she had still managed to lose weight off her already thin frame. She hadn't worn that dress since the girls were young.

Inviting him into the house, she asked if he wanted a glass of wine and moved to the kitchen to open a bottle of red. It was his favorite, which she had learned one night a week ago.

"And who's this gorgeous girl?" he asked as Rose moved to smell the situation.

"This is Rose," said Caroline, pouring the wine.

It made her heart explode watching him rub Rose's ears and tell her how pretty she was. He always loved dogs, and they always brought out his silliness.

"Shall we sit outside?" she asked.

The two then spent the next few hours chatting, going through two bottles of wine and ordering a pizza like they were in school again. After they had caught each other up on their lives, he asked her the question she had been dreading.

"What do you think really happened? Do you think anything was going on between the two of them that led to this?" he asked.

By this point, she was buzzed and tired. She kept staring at his full lips and white teeth. She took a sip of wine and looked to the sky.

"I don't know," she said. "I really don't."

* * * * *

During the visit, Officer Kelly had met Officer McKenna, who told him more about the family and the times he had visited there when Caroline first called the police.

"And there was a scratch?" asked Officer Kelly.

"Yes," Officer McKenna replied. "A big one along the door. It looked new. Don't know what it was from or how it got there. It had like an orange tint to it."

Throughout the services, Officer Kelly watched Caroline, who appeared pleasant yet sad. She bobbed around at both receptions offering guests more food or wine. Yet, at times she'd hide her face and he could tell she was crying.

But the biggest surprise of all was a man who stayed by her side throughout the services.

"What's his name?" Officer Kelly asked Officer McKenna.

"I think his name is Matt, and he's a college friend who came up to help out," Officer McKenna answered.

"He seems awfully friendly," said Officer Kelly. "Like a *really* good college friend."

"I think they dated. I heard someone talking about it," said Officer McKenna. He smiled as a woman walked up to stand by his side. He introduced her to Officer Kelly. "This is Maria," he said.

"Nice to meet you," replied Officer Kelly, shaking the woman's hand. "So, they dated back in college and now he's here at the funeral?"

"Suppose so, kind of weird. This whole thing is fucking weird," said Officer McKenna.

Maria hit him on the arm. "I don't think it's weird," she said. "I think it's nice. Rumor downtown is they did date in college and he came from California a week or so ago to help her through this. Really sweet of him. I met him, and he seems like a nice guy. Molly, Caroline's next-door neighbor, says he sometimes stays the night. Maybe Caroline needs the protection and the comfort."

Officer Kelly pulled out his phone and made a note. Something in his gut told him to.

CHAPTER 44

NEWBURYPORT, MASSACHUSETTS

Friday, November 26

Time can play tricks on people. Sometimes it moves quickly, leaving one to wonder where it all went. Sometimes it moves so slow that every second feels like a day. Caroline thought a lot about time now. Especially since it was time to put up the Christmas tree.

In holidays past, on the day after Thanksgiving, she and Greg would drag a hungover Noel and the two girls into the car and drive to cut a tree down at a local farm. Caroline would make a huge breakfast and always packed coffees to go for their outing.

The group would fight about the best choice, but it always seemed Noel got to pick the final tree. Arriving home, they'd put it up and spend the rest of the day decorating the tree and shopping online.

But this year, the girls decided to go home Thanksgiving night. Both had new boyfriends whom they had brought for dinner, joining their mother and Matt. In the car on the way to dinner, Amanda's boyfriend had asked if Matt was their mother's boyfriend.

"No," snapped Jackie.

"Well, kind of," replied Amanda.

The two had different opinions on this man being in their mother's life now. They had met him over the summer and knew the two had dated in college, and that he had been spending more time here now that he was retired. Their mother was different with Matt than what she had been with their father. She smiled and laughed and placed her hand on Matt's arm as they cooked together and drank red wine.

This year's Thanksgiving dinner felt cold as the table of six tried to make small talk over the food, weather, and politics. Caroline had placed a picture of Greg and Noel by the table, yet no one mentioned them. They did, however, all feel their stares as they ate.

When Matt and Caroline ventured into the kitchen to clean and the boyfriends moved to the living room to watch football, Jackie hit Amanda's arm.

"This is so fucking weird," she said. "This Matt guy being here and no mention about Dad or Noel. I talked to that Maine cop the other day like I told you. He called me and was asking some questions about nothing based on shit Molly had been gossiping about at the funeral. I just can't get it out of my head."

"Yeah, he called me, too. Just yesterday," said Amanda. "I never realized it until today when I saw Molly outside. Don't you think she kind of looks like Noel?"

"Yeah, I guess. Kind of. But this cop guy thinks that maybe Mom and Matt had something to do with this. Do you think that's true?" Jackie asked.

"No," Amanda replied flatly.

"Who wants pie?" asked Caroline, walking into the living room.

The boyfriends both said yes. She then looked to Jackie and Amanda, who both smiled.

"Okay, I'll cut four slices," she said and disappeared back into the kitchen.

"Mom does seem different now. Happier," said Amanda, looking at her sister. "I wonder why she wasn't more like this with Dad."

"I miss Dad," replied Jackie. "I'm sure you probably don't and miss Noel only, but I miss Dad."

"Jesus," snapped Amanda. "I miss them both."

* * * * *

Time had gone by since the murders and no one had answers. Caroline had spent months talking to investigators and lawyers, making trips to and from Maine, where she and Marigold had developed a friendship over cigarettes and whiskey. Caroline had been up the previous week with Matt, and Marigold mentioned her daughter and boyfriend were coming up the next day for the holiday week.

"Do you like this guy?" Marigold had asked as the two walked from crime scene to crime scene. This had become part of their routine.

Caroline felt a bit embarrassed about it, but Marigold had filled a void that was left with Noel's absence.

"I kind of do," she said, feeling free by hearing the words. "I used to think he was 'the one' when we were in school and then when he left me, I started dating Greg and one thing led to another and boom, I was married with kids."

Marigold could sense and see the change in Caroline. She was warmer now, more open.

"What if he leaves again?" Marigold asked.

"But what if he doesn't?" said Caroline, her blue eyes shining.

CHAPTER 45

MOUNT KATAHDIN, MAINE

Wednesday, December 1, at 6:45 p.m.

Marigold took a deep puff of her cigarette and chased the smoke down into her lungs with a swallow of whiskey. Rocking back and forth on the porch, she looked over the backyard and the leaves gracing the ground. Her daughter and boyfriend had left a few days prior, and the twins were still with her. Thanksgiving had gone well and she had enjoyed her time with Caroline.

Closing her eyes now, Marigold imagined the bodies and how Greg's face looked. She still wondered what he was like in real life. He looked handsome and nice, like a banker. She imagined him greeting customers as they walked into the bank with a warm smile and a friendly comment about the day or a question about their family.

Noel, though, she imagined as a bitch, a power-hungry woman looking to dominate some sort of corporation. She did this often but knew otherwise from her conversations with Caroline. Their two faces would enter her mind throughout the day and in her dreams. She wondered what they were like alive.

The last time she and Officer Kelly talked, he told her it was normal for these thoughts and dreams to continue on and it may be a while before she felt "back to normal," whatever that meant. That was almost six months ago.

Marigold even imagined seeing Caroline walking back and forth at the crime scenes and up and down the street with her grown twin girls trailing behind her in the same way that Iris's twins followed her.

Now when she cleaned the rooms at the inn, she'd glance out the window imagining that the plastic bag was still there holding the woman's body. Her thoughts ventured into darker places of who would want to kill them and why. Were they together, or were they friends?

Throwing her cigarette out into the yard, she heard the twins yelling at each other about the TV. Both seemed more on edge, and she wondered if they could sense her uneasiness or if it was due to their mother leaving them with her again with no true reunion in sight.

They yelled again.

"Kids," Marigold screamed. "Do I need to fucking come in there?"

"No, Grandma," Amelia chirped. "Harold and I will play nice."

"You better," Marigold responded and shook her head.

Taking another sip of whiskey, she shut her eyes and saw the two dead faces again.

"What did you both do?" she said softly to herself.

She imagined them stealing money from a bank customer, or embezzling money from a corporation and someone found out and wanted them dead. Someone insanely cruel and unforgiving and who knew Maine and Mount Katahdin.

Marigold wondered if the killer had stayed at the inn and if she had cleaned his room. She had made her mind up that it was a man and not a woman as she watched Officer Kelly and the other police officers walk around the pond and trash bag. It had to have been a man who dumped part of the woman by the pond and the man and the other part of her up the street.

"Amelia, you are such a bitch," screamed Harold, jolting Marigold out of her daydream.

"Jesus fucking Christ," she screamed. "What the shit are you kids doing in there?"

Amelia stuck her head out of the screen door. Her hair was a mess with a half-pigtail on one side and the other scraggly and undone.

"Child, when was the last time you took a shower?" she asked. Amelia shrugged.

"Go get a bath ready and I'll be in to make sure you don't drown in the tub. Don't get shit all around the bathroom again," snapped Marigold.

Amelia nodded and disappeared back into the house. Marigold pulled another cigarette from the box. Reaching for her lighter, she called for Harold.

"Yes, Grandma?" he asked innocently, sticking his head out the door.

Marigold put the filter in her mouth and lit it with the antique lighter she had found by the pond years before.

"Boy, why are you driving your sister and me crazy? What's going on with you?" she asked.

He shrugged and came to stand next to her on the porch.

"Can't you talk?" Marigold pressed. "Is this because of your momma leaving again?"

She often wondered if the stress of their mother coming in and out of their lives like this was more harmful than helpful.

Harold danced around nervously. Marigold hated that such a good-looking boy was going to grow up with such an old man name. But her daughter loved it. It was Marigold's father's name and Iris wanted to keep it alive. She often joked that she wanted to keep Harold as a name alive in the family like Marigold wanted to keep the names of flowers alive. That was a tradition that Iris stopped, but Harold was something she wanted to hang on to.

Grabbing his hand, she pulled him in front of her.

"Listen, I know there's some bad stuff happening. But if something's wrong, you gotta tell me. You can tell family. Now, what's going on that's got you and your sister acting like little assholes these days?" Marigold pressed.

He shrugged again. "Grandma, I don't know. Momma said she was going to bring us back to Boston with her but then she left again with Sammy. And without us. I want Momma to come back and get us like she says," Harold replied.

Marigold knew that their mother did this on the phone. She had listened in on the landline a few times when Iris had called and promised her kids she'd be coming up to get them to bring them back to Boston. But she never did.

"Harold, come here," she said and drew the boy into a hug.

She smelled his hair. It smelled and looked like sunshine.

"I'm sorry your momma told you this, but you're still going to stay here with me. And if you're staying here with me, you need to be good to your sister, okay?" comforted Marigold.

Harold pulled away and nodded.

"Now go back in the house. I'm going to help your sister with her bath," said Marigold.

Marigold dropped the cigarette that had been smoldering in one hand while Harold ventured back into the house. Getting up, she followed behind him. She went into the bathroom, where Amelia was lining up the makeup that her mother had brought her as a gift.

"Why'd you get all that stuff out?" Marigold huffed.

"I like it, Grandma," Amelia answered, pulling more stuff out of the pink cosmetic bag. Amelia then tipped the bag over, spilling out a few lipsticks from the Dollar Store, followed by a few nail polishes.

Marigold's heart fluttered. "Baby, what's this?" she said, reaching for one of the nail polish bottles.

"Momma gave me that one, too. Isn't it pretty?" Amelia answered.

Pulling it toward her face, Marigold twisted the bottle between her thin fingers. Looking back at her granddaughter, she turned pale.

"When did your momma give you this?" Marigold asked.

"A few days ago," Amelia answered and began to spin around.

Marigold looked down at the nail polish in her hand. It was bright orange.

CHAPTER 46

NEWBURYPORT, MASSACHUSETTS

Thursday, December 2, at 3:02 p.m.

It was a few days into December. Caroline was adding more decorations to her small, fake tree in the living room. Matt was in California with his kids for the week. She missed him but was happy for the break and the alone time.

He was spending so much time with her that she sometimes wanted a breather and time to still mourn without his concerned eyes watching over her. When he was there over Thanksgiving, after her girls had left, Matt wrapped his arms around her in the kitchen and swayed.

"I'm sorry I left you like that in college. I did love you. But I was a dumb kid and hated that school and just had to leave," he cooed into her ear. "I love you now and I loved you then."

She gushed inside with happiness and put the dish down that she had been wiping, turning so her lips could meet his. "I love you, too," she said, pressing her lips to his.

That moment was now her favorite, with that time in Vermont coming in at a close second.

While she was happy with this grownup Matt who listened to her and talked about his feelings and played with the dog, she knew what people thought. Molly was always coming over asking her about it. Caroline then heard that Molly would be in town telling people how strange it was that Caroline had moved on so quickly with the murderer of her husband and friend still at-large.

Caroline, for once in her life, didn't care what people thought. She was enjoying Matt regardless of her grief and was trying to let the professionals figure out what happened. It was their job, not hers, to solve this crime. If often crossed her mind, though, what if Noel and Greg were watching her with Matt from beyond. What would they say?

As she added the final ornament, her phone rang, waking her from her Matt-soaked thoughts. Picking it up, she saw that it was Officer Kelly. She both loved and hated seeing his calls because she would feel optimistic that he was calling to confirm who the murderer was, followed by feeling disappointed that he had no new information at all.

"Hello, Officer," she said. "How was your Thanksgiving?"

"Good," he said shortly.

"We need you to come up to Maine," he said. "We've got a clue and need you to bring anything with Noel's DNA and your husband's. May not need it but may not hurt."

Caroline froze. "Do you have a lead?" she asked with a stern voice.

"I think we may," he said.

* * * * *

The next day, Caroline was sitting by the inn's front door with clothing and personal items from Greg and Noel in a plastic bag. Marigold sat in the chair next to her equally concerned. Neither spoke. Caroline thought it was odd that Marigold was being so cold to her.

A few moments later, Officer Kelly walked in the door with a few other officers behind him. He nodded at the women and they nodded back. Taking a seat, he began.

"I'm not sure what you both know," he said. "But Marigold found this bottle of nail polish with her granddaughter the other day. And it looks to be the same color as what was on Noel's nails."

Caroline's mouth dropped and she looked at Marigold who was now pale.

"Are you kidding me or is this a real clue?" asked Caroline, turning to face Officer Kelly.

"This is a real clue," he said. "Somehow, the little girl got ahold of this bottle."

Caroline was confused about what she was hearing, but also surprised by the now grownup tone in Officer Kelly. Over the months, he had been ridiculed by the media on his handling of the case and overall inexperience. Between that and the lawyers, he had been beaten down and was a colder, hollower version of his previous self.

"We did a rush DNA test and it does look like it has Noel's DNA in the bottle and around the brush," he explained. "We want to check further based on the samples that you brought. The little girl informed us that her mother gave her the bottle of nail polish."

"Are you saying that the little girl had something to do with this?" asked Caroline.

"No, ma'am," said Officer Kelly. "We think her mother did and possibly the mother's boyfriend. They were up here the same weekend your husband and friend were found. He has a record of petty theft and crimes, but we do think they could be tied to the murders."

Marigold began to cry.

* * *

Marigold knew that something wasn't right with Sammy and that Iris had been hiding something. She could tell by how quiet her daughter was and by how tired she looked. She wasn't herself anymore.

And when she saw the nail polish, she knew she had to call Officer Kelly because something didn't feel right. When Marigold told him on the phone what she had found, he had been annoyed. But after some pleading and begging, she convinced him to test the bottle, knowing that it may be a clue, as much as that pained her.

"So now what happens?" Caroline asked glancing around the room.

"Well, we're going to need a few things. Marigold, can you call your daughter and try to get her and the boyfriend up here? Our plan is for you to get them here and then we can question them on this," Officer Kelly explained.

Marigold nodded through her tears, thinking how much this would impact the twins.

"How soon do you think you can do that?" Officer Kelly asked.

"I'll call now," Marigold said. "What should I say is the reason?"

"Tell her one of the children is sick," said Officer Kelly. "And that she needs to come right away."

Marigold sniffled and reached for her phone.

"Call Iris," she instructed her smartphone.

"Hi, Mom. What's going on? Are the kids okay?" said Iris on the other line.

Marigold drew a large breath in.

"No, our baby boy is sick. I need you to come on back up here. I'm not sure what to do about him," Marigold explained.

After some back and forth, Marigold's convincing finally worked.

"She's on her way," she finally said, putting the phone back in her pocket.

"Now what?" asked Caroline.

"Now we wait for them to get here," replied Officer Kelly. "It could be a while. Marigold, let me know when they get up to the house and I'll come up to escort them down to the station."

He left the room, leaving Marigold and Caroline alone. Marigold got up and walked out of the room without saying a word.

* * * * *

Caroline was now sitting alone with an unopened book on her lap, looking over to where part of Noel was found. Sometimes she'd walk to where Greg was found and tell him about the girls and life, but she always avoided mentioning Matt.

After a few hours and several chapters in, Caroline's phone buzzed. Looking down, there was a message from Marigold saying that Iris and Sammy had arrived and that she had let Officer Kelly know. He was on his way to her house.

"Should I come?" wrote Caroline.

"Meet us down at the station," replied Marigold.

"I can't imagine how you must feel. Stay strong, though," wrote Caroline.

Marigold replied with a heart emoji. Caroline felt terrible for Marigold, along with managing her own grief. She couldn't understand why Iris or Sammy would have done this to her family.

On her way to the station, she got a call from Matt. She declined it as she wasn't quite sure what to say to him about what was happening. Caroline debated calling the girls to let them know but decided against that too since there was really nothing yet to say.

CHAPTER 47

MOUNT KATAHDIN, MAINE

Friday, December 3, at 4:16 p.m.

Sitting across from the couple, Officer Kelly was unsure how to start. He knew his career was hanging on this moment with the discovery of DNA matching Noel to the nail polish bottle that Marigold's granddaughter had.

Marigold was sitting outside the conference room door. Caroline was by her side silently holding her hand.

Inside the room, Officer Kelly reviewed some papers in an attempt to make Sammy and Iris nervous. It was working as Sammy fidgeted and Iris's hands tapped the table.

"Why are we here?" Iris finally asked. "My mom said my baby was sick, which was a lie. She's always such a fucking liar. Why are we here? For real?"

Officer Kelly looked up and sighed. "You want to tell me?" he asked. "Make this easier and get the guilt off your back?"

"What? Is this some sort of sick joke?" Iris snapped.

He could tell she was her mother's daughter.

"I want to know what's going on and now," Iris demanded.

"And so do I," he pressed. "Why don't you tell me how you know those two people your mom found?"

"We don't," said Sammy coyly. "We don't know those people that were found up here in this dump."

"Then why does your daughter have the nail polish bottle that matches the color and the DNA of the woman who was found?" he asked.

Officer Kelly was tired of pretending. He was tired of this case. He was tired of the media.

"What?" asked Iris, whose face began to flush.

"You heard me," said Officer Kelly. "Let's just get to the point and quit the fucking act."

"This is no fucking act," screamed Iris. "I want a fucking lawyer."

"Can you even afford that?" Officer Kelly asked.

Sammy snickered.

"Can you afford it?" Officer Kelly asked, turning to him.

"Nah, man. We don't have anything to do with this," said Sammy. "This is some bullshit. Are you sure her crazy momma didn't kill those people over at the inn and drag them up the street?"

"Why would she do that?" asked Officer Kelly.

"Man, I dunno," said Sammy shrugging. "She's a crazy bitch, too."

The two began to bicker, annoying Officer Kelly. He instructed an officer to escort Sammy out of the room so he could speak with Iris alone.

Officer Kelly began questioning Iris on her whereabouts during the time of the crimes. He could tell she was starting to crack without having Sammy by her side.

"We know you were up here the weekend they were killed. Your mom told us that. So, you would have been driving through Newburyport on your way up here around the time that they disappeared on that Saturday night, yes?" he asked.

Iris was even more flushed now and couldn't sit still in her seat. Sweat began to trickle down her forehead.

"I don't know," she replied.

Officer Kelly was getting annoyed. "Listen," he finally said. "You've got something to do with this. Your mother and kids have suffered enough. That woman out in the hall has suffered enough. Cut the shit and just tell me what the fuck happened." He slammed his hand on the desk.

Iris began to cry. He knew he had her now.

"Tell me what happened," he said in a softer tone.

"It was an accident," she began. The tears began to flow.

Officer Kelly couldn't believe it. She had cracked. "Just tell me what happened, and it will be okay," Officer Kelly comforted and cooed. "Just tell me what happened."

Iris began to cry more. He let her, not saying a word.

"Sammy needed money," she began. "And this guy in Boston was talking to him about knocking off this couple. This guy's aunt and uncle. He was going to pay Sammy a part of the insurance money. They were rich, living up in Newburyport and all."

"Then what happened, Iris?" he asked.

"We planned to come up and see my mom so we could whack them and then hide out up here for a few days," she explained. "But it went all wrong."

"How so?" asked Officer Kelly. "What happened?"

"We had driven up and down the street where they lived a few times looking for the right house," she said. "And we thought we had them spotted. But then there were like two sets of people who all looked alike and we got confused. Sammy said it was time to act and we were in his old van. We totally looked out of place. We saw the couple walking down the driveway and some chick over by the water with a dog. We pulled up quick in the driveway in the front of the house and Sammy told me to pull the gun on them and get them in the van."

Officer Kelly nodded, not wanting to break her concentration and story.

"I had the gun and told them to get the fuck in," she said. "They looked at me so confused. I knew it was the wrong couple. They didn't look like the ones in the pictures I saw on social media. I knew it, but Sammy told me to shut up and to get them in the van. The woman had red hair like in the photo and they both looked kind of old."

Officer Kelly nodded again, surprised at how Iris was giving him every detail.

"Then what happened?" he asked.

"I got out and put the gun to the man's chest. He got in the van then like no big deal, like a pussy. You could tell he was really scared. But there was no one around to help," she said. "But that fucking bitch ran toward the house and around the back. She ran like hell for an old chick. I ran to grab the woman. She almost made it into the fucking house but fell at the doorstep. I grabbed her leg and her fucking nails were digging in by the door. But Sammy came up behind me and grabbed her, too, after he had handcuffed the man in the van. We dragged her in and shut the door and took off with the two in the back of the van."

Officer Kelly let out a breath. This was part of the story, but he needed more.

"Then what happened?" he asked.

She shook her head.

"I was looking at them and knew it was the wrong people. They kind of looked younger than the picture we had from the guy Sammy knew, even for old people. I asked them, 'Are you Molly and Frank?' and they said no. But it was too fucking late. Sammy slapped the steering wheel and yelled, 'Fuck.' We knew we had to kill them. We just knew it," she explained.

"Keep going," encouraged Officer Kelly.

"We drove and drove and drove," she said. "We had nowhere else to go and my fucking mom kept texting me about the kids and to get up here. They were begging us to let them go. But we knew we couldn't. The guy kept saying he loved his wife and family and they wouldn't tell no one. But I've seen enough movies and that's a lie. When we got up here, we pulled into an old logger shack down the road. No one was there, so we got to work. Sammy got out of the van and uncuffed the guy and pulled him out. Then, he shot the guy in the head," Iris continued.

Officer Kelly felt sick. This was it.

"Then what happened?" he asked, still surprised at how easily she had cracked.

"The woman started freaking out and somehow weaseled out of the handcuffs and got out of the van," she said. "She tried to come at me after we shot the man, and Sammy hit her and knocked her down. Sammy jumped on top of her and strangled her," she explained.

There were no more tears. There was no emotion. There was just the story.

"Okay, how did the woman get cut in half?" Officer Kelly asked.

"That's the fucking thing that I wanted to kill Sammy myself about, fucking idiot," she said. "He didn't think that through so now my mother's up my ass texting me about where we were and I'm in some fucking shack with two dead bodies and an idiot for a boyfriend." She huffed. "Can I smoke in here?" she asked.

Just like her mother, thought Officer Kelly. He nodded, as he needed her to keep talking.

Iris lit a cigarette and continued talking. "I told Sammy we needed to get rid of the bodies and maybe we should cut them up and drop them around the mountain. Animals would eat them, you know? Maybe the park rangers would find parts eventually. Getting rid of the evidence. He went back into the shack to see what he could find. He came out with a fucking chainsaw. I nearly puked," she said. "I told him to try a knife first. He tried. But then he fired up the chainsaw and went right to it. We were in the woods and I knew no one would see us. The first attempt he sucked at, but then he was able to weasel it around and slide the blade right through her, clean cut," said Iris and took a puff of her cigarette.

"Then what?" Officer Kelly asked.

"We knew we had to get rid of the bodies and decided to leave the man whole because we were in a rush, so we thought we'd dump one part of her in the lake and her body would be eaten up or whatever and then the rest along the road. We got freaked out and didn't cut her up as much as we wanted. And we didn't want blood all over the van, so he got a trash bag out of the shed and we put one half in it. Sammy was getting all nervous, so we decided to go dump the top of her out the back of the van and then do the rest later," she said and took another puff. She paused. "I'm totally fucked, aren't I?" she asked.

"Not sure," said Officer Kelly. "Tell me what happened next."

"Once we put the chick in the two bags in the van next to the man, we headed down to the fucking lake and pulled up. I could see my mom's car and I thought I saw the kids. I got nervous that they were going to see. I told Sammy we had to wait. Later that night, we went out and dropped the chick. Sammy was getting really nervous and wanted to get rid of everything. I told him he was a dumb shit. He told me I was fucking dumb and we got in a fight," Iris continued.

"And you decided to get rid of both bodies down the street?" asked Officer Kelly.

She nodded in agreement.

"At that point, I didn't fucking care. I thought maybe a bear would come down and eat them. But Sammy is so fucking weak that he only dragged the bodies into the woods a little bit. I was pissed. We headed home and then he texted this guy about his fucking mistake," she explained.

"What's the guy's name? The one in Boston who had you guys do this?" asked Officer Kelly.

Iris thought for a moment. "I don't know his fucking name. I know he wanted money and had a bad photo, an old one of his aunt and uncle. We got confused. We fucked up and got the wrong people. I knew it. I found the nail polish in the back of the van the other fucking day and gave it to my kid. Now what?" she asked.

"I don't know," said Officer Kelly. It was the truth. He wasn't sure, but he had a full confession on tape.

"I'll be back," he said and left the room leaving the other officer to keep watch.

When he opened the door, Caroline and Marigold looked up at him. He nodded.

"She and Sammy did it," he said and kept walking toward the group of officers nearby. He needed all the help he could get to figure out what would happen next.

Marigold screamed and Caroline reached out to hold her. They had the murderers. But she wanted to understand why. Why her two people out of everyone in the world?

A few hours later, once Sammy and Iris were locked in cells and Marigold had been sedated and driven home, Officer Kelly sat across from Caroline at the station. He was unsure of what to tell her but thought it was best that he was honest.

"Listen," he began. "This is hard to say."

"Please just say it," Caroline said. She had yet to talk to her daughters or Matt. She wanted to tell them the answer when she did.

"It sounds like it was a murder for hire and they were after your neighbors but got confused. Mistaken identity," he said.

Caroline's mouth dropped. Officer Kelly told her more about the man in Boston who they were trying to identify. He thought it would be easy since they knew who the targets were.

"Mistaken identity? They wanted Frank and Molly?" she asked, not being able to believe it.

Officer Kelly nodded.

"They wanted my neighbors?" she asked still in disbelief.

Officer Kelly nodded again.

Caroline sat back and stared out the window, her mind blank with shock.

CHAPTER 48

NEWBURYPORT, MASSACHUSETTS

Wednesday, April 27, at 1:22 p.m.

onths later, Caroline was walking into the house with Matt behind her. The scratch was still there. The verdict had come in as guilty for both people. For Sammy, first degree and for Iris second degree murder. That's all Caroline remembered hearing.

During the trial, they heard from park rangers and police from Massachusetts, New Hampshire, and Maine. Toll pass records had been reviewed from the van passing from state to state along with cell phone records and tower pings. DNA reports were reviewed, plus testimonials. Frank and Molly took turns on the stand, too. Their nephew was being tried separately in a few months.

On the stand, each had talked about their relationships with both Greg and Noel. Marigold shared memories, through her tears and sobs, of her daughter and how shocked she was that she would have done this. She told the court how she wanted to be a good mom and didn't know where she went wrong.

Neither Sammy nor Iris showed remorse while hearing from the family, Marigold, or Officer Kelly when they spoke. When Dr. Isaac took the stand and discussed the bodies, Iris slumped in her chair, closing her eyes and simply looking bored. But the judge, jury, and the families had their answers on how this happened and why.

Molly and Frank had moved out of the house next door a few weeks earlier, shocked to learn that their nephew, Luke, had tried to have them murdered for money. It was too much for them to handle, having to look at Caroline each day knowing her family was gone because of Luke and his greed.

Caroline was tempted to sell her house, but she still had happy memories there. Matt was talking about moving to Newburyport to be closer to her and the idea made her giggle like a child, but she still felt guilty and wondered what Greg would have thought.

On the drive home from Portland, where the trial had been held, she and the girls shared memories of Greg and Noel. She felt closer to them now than she ever had before.

"Want some wine?" Matt asked.

She nodded. And then it occurred to her that she had never read the note she found under Greg's desk so many months before. It was still in the top desk drawer. Kicking off her heels, she wondered what it said.

Walking down the hall, her heart palpitated. Maybe it was the social media password they had searched for all along. She entered his office and shut the door, leaving Rose in the hall, and walked to the desk. She pulled the chair out, sat down, and opened the drawer.

Pulling out the note, she unfolded it carefully and took a deep breath. At the top, she noticed the date. It was written a few weeks before Greg and Noel disappeared. She began to read:

Dear Caroline,

For years I have loved you. From the first day I saw you, I loved you. I love you and the girls more than life. We have had a beautiful life.

Yet, throughout the years, I could feel that you didn't love me the way I loved you.

It broke my heart. I could never tell you as I don't think you would have cared.

While Noel and I resisted our feelings for years for your sake, over the last year or so, we decided that life is too short to be unhappy. We've decided to move to Florida together and start fresh. I think you'll be happier without me, but maybe not without her.

Please understand. We are both so sorry about this.

Love always,
Greg and Noel

Caroline could feel the tears bubbling up behind her eyes. They weren't tears of sadness but of confusion. There *had* been something going on. She had believed them all along that nothing was there but friendship. They had lied to her. They both had. And now they were both dead and together.

"Babe, come have some wine," Matt shouted from the kitchen.

Caroline refolded the note and placed it back in the top drawer. Getting up, she wandered down the hall. Matt handed her a glass of wine, and she reached for it and put it on the counter to free her arms to embrace him.

"I love you more than life," she said and kissed his cheek. She'd burn the letter once Matt left so no one else had to know.

ACKNOWLEDGEMENTS

Thank you to my parents, Mary and James Rymsha.

Thank you to Lt. Kevin F. Donovan of the Amesbury Police Department in Amesbury, Massachusetts, for aiding in my research.